Watch Manufacturing Companies Of Switzerland, including: The Swatch Group, Rolex, International Watch Company, Tissot, Waltham Watch Company, Waltham International, Breitling, Omega Sa, Tag Heuer, Patek Philippe & Co., Vacheron Constantin, Piaget Sa

Hephaestus Books

Contents

Articles

References

The Swatch Group

The Swatch Group

Type	Publicly-traded limited company (SIX: UHR [1], UHRN [2])
Industry	Luxury goods, accessories
Founded	1983
Founder(s)	Nicolas Hayek
Headquarters	Biel, Switzerland
Key people	Nayla Hayek (Chairman), Nick Hayek, Jr. (CEO)
Products	Watches, jewellery, electronic systems for timekeeping
Revenue	CHF 5.142 billion (2009)
Operating income	CHF 903 million (2009)
Profit	CHF 763 million (2009)
Employees	23,560 (2009)
Website	www.swatchgroup.com [3]

The Swatch Group Ltd. (SIX: UHR [1], UHRN [2]) is a Swiss company and watch manufacturer. It was formed in 1983 through the merging of the two Swiss watch manufacturers ASUAG and SSIH, and took its present name in 1998 (formerly SMH Swiss Corporation for Microelectronics and Watchmaking Industries Ltd). The company is led by G. Nicolas (Nick) Hayek, Jr., son of the late co-founder and chairman Nicolas Hayek.

In 2007, gross sales were 5.94 billion CHF. The Swatch Group has around 23,600 employees.

History

The Swatch Group formed from two financially troubled predecessor companies:

- SSIH originated in 1930 with the merger of the Omega and Tissot companies. Swiss watch quality was high, but new technology such as the Hamilton Electric watch introduced in 1957 and the Bulova Accutron tuning fork watch introduced in 1961 presaged increasing high technology competition.

In the late 1970s SSIH became insolvent due in part to a recession and in part to heavy competition from inexpensive Asian made quartz crystal watches. These difficulties occurred even though it had become Switzerland's largest and the world's third largest producer of watches. Its creditor banks assumed control in 1981.

- ASUAG, formed in 1931, was the world's largest producer of watch movements and the parts thereof (Balance wheels, Balance Springs (Spiral), Assortments, Watch Stones ("rubis"). ASUAG had also integrated an array of Watch brand in 1972 into a sub holding company, General Watch Co.

ASUAG failed similarly in 1982.

Both groups were reorganized and merged into SSIH/ASUAG Holding Company in 1983. Taken private, in 1985, by then CEO Nicolas Hayek, with the understanding of the Swiss Banks and the financial assistance of a group of Swiss private investors, it was renamed SMH in 1986, and ultimately Swatch Group Ltd in 1998.

The launch of the new Swatch brand "Swatch" watch in 1983, by the then ETA SA CEO Ernst Thomke and his young team of engineers, was marked by bold new styling and design. The quartz watch was redesigned for manufacturing efficiency and fewer parts. This combination of marketing and manufacturing expertise restored Switzerland as a major player in the world wristwatch market.

Brands

The Swatch Group owns several companies which do research (Asulab, EM Microelectronic-Marin, Oscilloquartz SA), produce movements (ETA SA, Valjoux, F. Piguet), produce pieces of watches (Comadur), and numerous watch brands which include Swatch, Flik Flak, Mido, Tissot, Calvin Klein, Certina, Pierre Balmain, Hamilton, Rado, Omega SA, Longines, Union Glashütte, Breguet, Blancpain, Jaquet Droz, Glashütte Original, Léon Hatot, Tiffany & Co., and Endura.

Flik Flak

Electronic Systems

The Swatch Group Electronic System [4] provides complete solutions by integrating the individual expertise of the following companies:

- EM Microelectronic-Marin [5]: Designs and produces ultra-low power, low voltage mixed-signal integrated circuits, LCD and modules. IC Product lines include RFID, microcontroller, smart card, ASIC, RTC, reset circuit, watchdog, LCD driver, opto ICs.
- Oscilloquartz SA : Produces and designs high precision frequency control products, including Cesium PRS, quartz crystal oscillator, OCXO, BVA & PRC, SSU (also called SASE, TSG or BITS), GPS based synchronisation products for the wireless and wired telecommunication infrastructure.
- Micro Crystal [6]: Produces miniature low power quartz crystals and small low power

oscillators. Focus is 32.768 kHz SMD and through hole crystals in miniature metal and ceramic package.

- Renata [7]: Develops and produces micro batteries. Product lines include button cells and rechargeable (Lithium Polymer) batteries. Primary batteries include Silver Oxide Lithium and Zinc-Air technologies.
- Lasag [8]: Offers solid-state lasers for precision welding, cutting, drilling and ablating of metals.

Once Again

The Nicolas G. Hayek Watchmaking School

The **Swatch Group** started offering their first class for aspiring watchmakers in September 2005. This school is based out of Miami, Florida. Another school is located in Okmulgee, Oklahoma. Other watchmaker schools outside the US are situated in Glashütte (Germany), Pforzheim (Germany), Kuala Lumpur (Malaysia) and Shanghai (China).

Internet Time and new technologies

In 1998, Swatch invented "Swatch Internet Time", intended as a global timesystem, which divides the day into 1000 "beats" in a single worldwide timezone.

In October 2004, Swatch introduced its first smart watch, the Paparazzi, based on Microsoft Corporation's SPOT (Smart Personal Objects Technology) technology.

Oscilloquartz SA, a company of the Swatch Group Electronic Systems, also produces NTP time server products.

Ventures

In 1994, Swatch entered into a joint venture with Germany's Daimler AG to produce the *Smart*, but they later withdrew from this project.

See also

- Pierre Jaquet-Droz

Further reading

- Mudambi, Ram, "Branding Time: Swatch and Global Brand Management" [9] - Temple University, Fox School of Business, Temple University IGMS Case Series No. 05-001, January 2005
- The Swatch Group Ltd., "History of the Swatch Group" [10]

External links

- Official website [11]
- Yahoo! - The Swatch Group Ltd. Company Profile [12]
- The Swatch Group History [13]

Rolex

Rolex

Type	Privately held company
Industry	Watch movement & case manufacturing
Founded	1905 by Hans Wilsdorf and Alfred Davis in London
Headquarters	Geneva, Switzerland
Key people	Bruno Meier (CEO), Michael Elms (CFO)
Products	Wristwatches, accessories
Revenue	£1.75 billion (US$3 billion) (SwFr3.02 billion) (2003 figures)
Employees	2,800
Website	Rolex.com [1]

Rolex SA is a Swiss manufacturer of high-quality, luxury wristwatches.

Rolex watches are popularly regarded as status symbols and *BusinessWeek* magazine ranks Rolex #71 on its 2007 annual list of the 100 most valuable global brands. Rolex is also the largest single luxury watch brand, producing about 2,000 watches per day, with estimated revenues of around US$3 billion (£1.75) (3.02 CHF billion) (2003 figures).

History

In 1905 Hans Wilsdorf and his brother-in-law Alfred Davis founded "Wilsdorf and Davis" in London. Their main business at the time was importing Hermann Aegler's Swiss movements to England and placing them in quality watch cases made by Dennison and others. These early wristwatches were sold to jewellers, who then put their own names on the dial. The earliest watches from Wilsdorf and Davis were usually hallmarked "W&D" inside the caseback.

In 1908 Wilsdorf registered the trademark "Rolex" and opened an office in La Chaux-de-Fonds, Switzerland. The company name "Rolex" was registered on 15 November 1915. The word was made up, but its origin is obscure. Wilsdorf was said to want his watch brand's name to be easily pronounceable in any language. He also thought that the name "Rolex" was onomatopoeic, sounding like a watch being wound. It was also short enough to fit on the face of a watch. One story, never confirmed by Wilsdorf, is that the name came from the French phrase *horlogerie exquise*, meaning "exquisite clockwork". The book *The Best of Time: Rolex Wristwatches: An Unauthorized History* by Jeffrey P. Hess and James Dowling says that the name was just made up.

In 1914 Kew Observatory awarded a Rolex watch a *Class A precision certificate*, a distinction which was normally awarded exclusively to marine chronometers.

In 1919 Wilsdorf moved the company to Geneva, Switzerland where it was established as the *Rolex Watch Company*. Its name was later changed to *Montres Rolex, SA* and finally *Rolex, SA*. The company moved out of the United Kingdom because taxes and export duties on the silver and gold used for the watch cases were driving costs too high.

Upon the death of his wife in 1944, Wilsdorf established the Hans Wilsdorf Foundation in which he left all of his Rolex shares, making sure that some of the company's income would go to charity. The company is still owned by a private trust and shares are not traded on any stock exchange.

In December 2008 the abrupt departure of Chief Executive Patrick Heiniger, for "personal reasons", was followed by a denial by the company that it had lost SwFr1 billion (approx £574 million, $900 million) invested with Bernard Madoff, the American asset manager who pleaded guilty to an approximately £30 billion worldwide Ponzi scheme fraud.

Innovations

Among the company's innovations are:

- The first wristwatch with an automatically changing date on the dial (Rolex Datejust, 1945)
- The first wristwatch with an automatically changing day and date on the dial (Rolex Day-Date)
- The first wristwatch case waterproof to 100 m (330 ft) (Rolex Oyster Perpetual Submariner, 1953)
- The first wristwatch to show two time zones at once (Rolex GMT Master, 1954)
- The first watchmaker to earn chronometer certification for a wristwatch

The Rolex Submariner Professional Date

Automatic movements

The first self-winding Rolex wristwatch was offered to the public in 1931, preceded to the market by Harwood which patented the design in 1923 and produced the first self-winding watch in 1928, powered by an internal mechanism that used the movement of the wearer's arm. This not only made watch-winding unnecessary, but kept the power from the mainspring more consistent resulting in more reliable time keeping.

Quartz movements

Rolex participated in the development of the original quartz watch movements. Although Rolex has made very few quartz models for its Oyster line, the company's engineers were instrumental in design and implementation of the technology during the late 1960s and early 1970s. In 1968, Rolex collaborated with a consortium of 16 Swiss watch manufacturers to develop the *Beta 21* quartz movement used in their Rolex *Quartz Date* 5100. Within about five years of research, design, and development, Rolex created the "clean-slate" 5035/5055 movement that would eventually power the Rolex *Oysterquartz*.

Water-resistant cases

Rolex was also the first watch company to create a wristwatch water resistant to 100 m (330 ft). Wilsdorf even had a specially made Rolex watch attached to the side of the Trieste bathyscaphe, which went to the bottom of the Mariana Trench. The watch survived and tested as having kept perfect time during its descent and ascent. This was confirmed by a telegram sent to Rolex the following day saying "Am happy to confirm that even at 11,000 metres your watch is as precise as on the surface. Best regards, Jacques Piccard".

Collections

Rolex produced specific models suitable for the extremes of deep-sea diving, mountain climbing and aviation. Early sports models included the Rolex Submariner and the Rolex Oyster Perpetual Date Sea Dweller. The latter watch has a helium release valve, co-invented with Swiss watchmaker Doxa, to release helium gas build-up during decompression. The Explorer and Explorer II were developed specifically for explorers who would navigate rough terrain, such as the world famous Mount Everest expeditions. The most iconic model is the Rolex GMT Master, which was originally developed in 1954 at the request of Pan Am Airways to assist its pilots with the problem of crossing multiple time zones when on transcontinental flights (GMT standing for Greenwich Mean Time).

Certified chronometers

Rolex is the largest manufacturer of Swiss made certified chronometers. In 2005 more than half the annual production of COSC certified watches were Rolexes. To date, Rolex still holds the record for the most certified chronometer movements in the category of wristwatches.

Ceramic bezels

The company is now starting to introduce ceramic bezels across the range of professional sports watches. They are available on the Submariner and GMT Master II models. The ceramic bezel is not influenced by UV-light and is very scratch resistant.

Watch models

Rolex has three watch lines: *Oyster Perpetual*, *Professional* and *Cellini* (the Cellini line is Rolex's line of 'dressy' watches) and the primary bracelets for the Oyster line are named *Jubilee*, *Oyster* and *President.*

Rolex Daytona stainless steel (ref. 116520)

Modern Rolex models

- Air-King
- Date
- Datejust
- Datejust II
- Datejust Turn-O-Graph
- Lady Datejust Pearlmaster
- Daytona
    - Paul Newman Daytona
- Day-Date
- Day-Date II
- Day-Date Oyster Perpetual
- Explorer
- Explorer II
- GMT Master II
- Masterpiece
- Milgauss
- Oysterquartz
- Sea Dweller
- Sea Dweller DeepSea

Rolex Sea Dweller Deepsea with 3,900m depth rating (ref. 116660)

- Submariner
- Yacht-Master
- Yacht-Master II

Rolex Yacht-Master

Cellini models

- Quartz Ladies
- Quartz Mens
- Cellinium
- Cestello Ladies
- Cestello Mens
- Danaos Mens
- Prince

Rolex Daytona chronograph stainless steel, white dial (ref. 6263)

Tudor

Rolex sells less expensive watches under the Tudor brand name, which was introduced by Rolex founder Hans Wilsdorf in 1946. While still sold in Europe and the Far East, American sales of the Tudor line were discontinued in 2004.

Pricing

Rolex watches vary in price according to the model and the materials used. In the UK, the retail price for the highly sought-after stainless steel 'Pilots' range (such as the GMT Master II) starts from GBP £4,300. Diamond inlay watches go for considerably more.

Notable owners

- Che Guevara wore a Rolex GMT Master (stolen by CIA agent Félix Rodríguez, who was a witness to his execution).
- The Rolex Submariner has appeared in eleven James Bond movies. Rolex declined to give the film company a wristwatch *gratis* during the making of *Dr. No*, the first of the series in 1962, so the film's producer Cubby Broccoli lent Sean Connery his own (a Rolex Submariner on a black crocodile strap). Rolex supplied the wristwatches from the next film onwards.
- The ref 6542 stainless steel Rolex GMT Master was nicknamed the 'Pussy Galore', after the character (played by Honor Blackman) in the 1964 James Bond movie *Goldfinger*, who wore this model of wristwatch.

- Roger Federer, a Swiss professional tennis champion, is among a number of people Rolex pays to advertise its watches.

Significant events

Rolex is the official time keeper of Wimbledon and The Australian Open tennis grand slams.

Jacques Piccard had a Rolex Sea Dweller Deep-Sea Special with him strapped to the outside of his submarine in 1960 during the Mariana Trench dive at a depth of 10916 metres (35814 ft).

Tenzing Norgay and other members of the Hillary expedition wore Rolex Oysters in 1953 at altitude 8,848 m on Mount Everest while there are attestations and speculation that Sir Edmund Hillary either carried a Smiths Deluxe or a Rolex to the summit, or both.

Mercedes Gleitze was the first British woman to swim the English Channel on 7 October 1927. But, as John E. Brozek (author of *The Rolex Report: An Unauthorized Reference Book for the Rolex Enthusiast*) points out in his article *"The Vindication Swim, Mercedes Gleitze and Rolex take the plunge"*, some doubts were cast on her achievement when a hoaxer claimed to have made a faster swim only four days later. To silence her critics, Mercedes Gleitze attempted a repeat swim on 21 October in the full glare of publicity, thus touted the *"Vindication Swim"*. Hans Wilsdorf knew a good marketing opportunity when he saw one and offered her one of the earliest Rolex Oysters if she would wear it during the attempt. After more than 10 hours, in water that was much colder than during her first swim, she was pulled from the sea semi-conscious seven miles short of her goal. It was during this swim where she wore the Rolex watch, contrary to popular opinion. Although she did not complete the second crossing, a journalist for The Times wrote "Having regard to the general conditions, the endurance of Miss Gleitze surprised the doctors, journalists and experts who were present, for it seemed unlikely that she would be able to withstand the cold for so long. It was a good performance". This silenced the doubters and Mercedes Gleitze was hailed as a heroine. As she sat in the boat, the same journalist made a discovery and reported it as follows: "Hanging round her neck by a ribbon on this swim, Miss Gleitze carried a small gold watch, which was found this evening to have kept good time throughout". When examined closely, the watch was found to be in perfect condition, dry inside and ticking away as if nothing had happened. One month later, on 24 November 1927, Wilsdorf launched the Rolex Oyster watch in the United Kingdom as the focal point of a full front page Rolex advert in the Daily Mail and the Rolex Oyster began its rise to fame.

It is widely known that the Omega Speedmaster Pro was the only watch approved by NASA for use on the Apollo moon flights. Its official status has led it be called the "Moonwatch." However, many students and collectors of space-flown timepieces are aware that Jack Swigert carried and/or wore a Rolex on the ill-fated Apollo 13 flight which never landed on the moon. In addition, Apollo 17 Astronaut Ron Evans' personal watch was a 1968-era Rolex Oyster Perpetual GMT-Master. He placed it into his Personal Preference Kit (PPK) which was taken to the moon by his crewmates Gene Cernan and Harrison Schmitt aboard the Lunar Module Challenger, while he orbited the moon in the Command

Module America. It remained on the moon for approximately seventy-five hours on the last manned lunar landing mission. This watch was sold at auction in 2009 for $131,450 through Heritage Auctions of Dallas.

Watches for POWs and help in the *Great Escape*

By the start of World War II, Rolex watches had already acquired enough prestige that British Royal Air Force pilot officers bought them to replace their inferior standard-issue watches. However, when captured and sent to POW camps, their watches were confiscated. When Hans Wilsdorf heard of this, he offered to replace all watches that had been confiscated and not require payment until the end of the war, if the officers would write to Rolex and explain the circumstances of their loss and where they were being held. Wilsdorf, who believed that "a British officer's word was his bond", was in personal charge of the scheme. As a result of this, an estimated 3,000 Rolex watches were ordered by British officers in the Oflag (prison camp for officers) VII B POW camp in Bavaria alone. This had the effect of raising the morale among the allied POW's because it indicated that Wilsdorf did not believe that the Nazis would win the war. American servicemen heard about this when stationed in Europe during WWII and this helped open up the American market to Rolex after the war.

On 10 March 1943, while still a prisoner of war, Corporal Clive James Nutting, one of the organizers of the Great Escape, ordered a stainless steel Rolex Oyster 3525 Chronograph (valued at a current equivalent of £1,200) by mail directly from Hans Wilsdorf in Geneva, intending to pay for it with money he saved working as a shoemaker at the camp. The watch (Rolex watch no. 185983) was delivered to Stalag Luft III on 10 July that year along with a note from Wilsdorf apologising for any delay in processing the order and explaining that an English gentleman such as Corporal Nutting "should not even think" about paying for the watch before the end of the war. Wilsdorf is reported to have been impressed with Nutting because, although not an officer, he had ordered the expensive Rolex 3525 Oyster chronograph while most other prisoners ordered the much cheaper Rolex Speed King model which was popular due to its small size. The watch is believed to have been ordered specifically to be used in the Great Escape when, as a chronograph, it could have been used to time patrols of prison guards or time the 76 ill-fated escapees through tunnel 'Harry' on 24 March 1944. Eventually, after the war, Nutting was sent an invoice of only £15 for the watch, due to currency export controls in England at the time. The watch and associated correspondence between Wilsdorf and Nutting were sold at auction for £66,000 in May 2007, while at an earlier auction on September 2006 the same watch fetched AUS$54,000. Nutting served as a consultant for both the 1950 film *The Wooden Horse* and the 1963 film *The Great Escape*. Both films were based on actual escapes which took place at Stalag Luft III.

Murder investigation

See also: Albert Johnson Walker

In a famous murder case the Rolex that a victim wore on his wrist eventually led to the arrest of his murderer. When a body was found in the English Channel in 1996 by a fisherman, a Rolex wristwatch was the only identifiable object on the body. Since the Rolex movement had a serial number and was engraved with special markings every time it was serviced, British police traced the service records from Rolex and Ronald Joseph Platt was identified as the owner of the watch and the victim of the murder. In addition British police were able to determine the date of death by examining the date on the watch calendar and since the Rolex movement had a reserve of two to three days of operation when inactive and it was fully waterproof, they were able to determine the time of death within a small margin of error..

Counterfeits

Rolex watches are frequently counterfeited, often illegally sold on the street and online.

Media

Rolex headquarters in Geneva

Rolex manufactory in Biel/Bienne

See also

- Rolex awards
- List of watch manufactures

External links

- Official website [1]

International Watch Company

International Watch Company

Type	Watch Maker
Industry	Watch Making
Founded	1868
Headquarters	Schaffhausen, Switzerland
Area served	Worldwide
Products	Watches
Employees	309
Parent	Richemont International SA
Website	www.iwc.ch [1]

International Watch Co, also known as **IWC**, is a high-end Swiss watch manufacturer located in Schaffhausen, Switzerland. IWC is an active member of the Federation of the Swiss Watch Industry FH.

Located in Schaffhausen, IWC Schaffhausen is notable for being the only major Swiss watch factory located in eastern Switzerland, as the majority of the well-known Swiss watch manufacturers are located in western Switzerland. Notwithstanding, the lingua franca of IWC is German.

Motto

IWC's motto is ***Probus Scafusia*** (L.), meaning "*good, solid craftsmanship from Schaffhausen*" and was established in 1903 as the "Official Motto".

History

Creation

In 1868, an American engineer and watchmaker Florentine Ariosto Jones (1841–1916) who had been a director of E. Howard & Co., in Boston, then America's leading watchmaking company, founded the International Watch Company with the intention of combining the craftsmanship of the Swiss with the modern engineering technology from the U.S. to manufacture movements and watch parts for the American market." At the time, wages in Switzerland were relatively low although there was a ready supply of skilled watchmaking labor" mainly carried out by people in their homes. Jones encountered opposition to his plans in French-speaking Switzerland because people feared for their jobs" and the work they did at home because Jones wanted to open a factory.

IWC Grande Complication

In 1850 the town of Schaffhausen was in danger of being left behind in the Industrial Age. It was at this stage that watch manufacturer and industrialist Johann Heinrich Moser stepped in and did the region a huge service. As a pioneer of *white coal*, he built Schaffhausen's first hydroelectric plant and laid the cornerstone for future industrialization." He probably met F.A. Jones in Le Locle and showed great interest in his plans. Together, they laid the foundations for the only watch manufacturers in north-eastern Switzerland: The International Watch Company in Schaffhausen.

Early stages

In 1869 F.A. Jones rented the first factory premises in an industrial building owned by J.H. Moser in Rheinstrasse. Very soon he had to rent further rooms in the *Oberhaus*, one of the oldest buildings in Schaffhausen. By 1874 plans were already being made for a new factory and a site was purchased from Moser's hydroelectric company which was directly adjacent to the banks of the Rhine and called the *Baumgarten*. Schaffhausen architect G. Meyer won the order to design and build the factory. A year later, in the spring of 1875, the construction work was completed. At first, 196 people worked in the 45 meter long factory, which could accommodate up to 300 workplaces.

IWC manufacture in Schaffhausen.

IWC and the Rauschenbach family

Johann Rauschenbach-Vogel, Chief Executive Officer and a machine manufacturer from Schaffhausen, took over the INTERNATIONALE UHRENFABRIK on 17 February 1880. Four generations of the Rauschenbach family owned IWC, with varying names.

The *Portuguese* series of watches

Only a year after the sale, Johannes Rauschenbach died. His son, Johannes Rauschenbach-Schenk, was 25 years old when he took over the UHRENFABRIK VON J. RAUSCHENBACH and ran it successfully until his own death on 2 March 1905.

Another significant role on the way to the company's success was played by Urs Haenggi from Nunningen in the canton of Solothurn. He had got to know the watch business in French-speaking Switzerland and France; in 1883 he joined IWC and stayed with the company for 52 years. He was responsible for getting factory operations up and running smoothly and acquiring new customers. He was also responsible for warding off the prospect of the outside interests acquiring IWC "in the interest of the noble Rauschenbach family".

After the death of J. Rauschenbach-Schenk in 1905, his wife, two daughters and their husbands, Ernst Jakob Homberger (director of G. Fischer AG in Schaffhausen) and Dr. Carl Jung (psychologist and psychiatrist), took over the watch factory as an open trading company by the name of the UHRENFABRIK VON J. RAUSCHENBACH'S ERBEN. E.J. Homberger was the only authorized signatory, Haenggi and Vogel were directors.

Following the death of his father-in-law, Ernst Jakob Homberger had a considerable influence on the Schaffhausen watchmaking company's affairs and guided it through one of the most turbulent epochs in Europe's history. Just before the world economic crisis, he took over as sole proprietor and renamed the company UHRENFABRIK VON ERNST HOMBERGER-RAUSCHENBACH, formerly INTERNATIONAL WATCH CO. His contribution was honored in 1952, when he was awarded an honorary doctorate by the University of St. Gallen. He died in 1955, aged 85 years.

Hans Ernst Homberger was the third and last of the Rauschenbach heirs to run the factory as a sole proprietor. He had joined his father's company in 1934 and took control after his death in April 1955. In 1957 he added a new wing to the factory and in the same year set up a modern pension fund for the staff. He bought new machines to meet new demands and continuously brought his production technology up to what were considered the very latest standards. He died in 1986 at the age of 77.

Prominent technicians

Technician Johann Vogel from Wangen an der Aare in Solothurn played an important role as technical director. He designed and developed IWC calibers until 1919.

In 1885, IWC manufactured the first digital watch based on a patent granted to an Austrian by the name of Pallweber. It was a simple design, but was unable to replace the traditional analogue display.

Electrical era

In 1888 electricity began to take over at the watch factory. J. Rauschenbach had a power line installed which supplied it with electricity. During the first few years the electrical power was probably used only for lighting purposes and the galvanic gold-plating of watch movement parts. Shortly before the turn of the century, the company started converting its production machines to electricity. An electric motor made by Brown, Boveri & Co. from Baden powered the engines in the factory, transmitting the energy via a complicated arrangement of shafts and drive belts in the factory workshops. These were later replaced during the 1930s with individually-powered machines.

1900-1960

During the period just before and after the First World War, E.J. Homberger devoted himself to devising and setting up social institutions. He extended the living quarters for factory employees and established a fund for widows and orphans. In 1929, the name of the fund was changed to the J.Rauschenbach Foundation and in 1949 he founded the Watch Company Welfare Foundation.

On April 1, 1944, as a result of a fatal error, Schaffhausen was bombed by the United States Army Air Force. The watch factory was hit by a bomb which failed to detonate after crashing through the rafters. The flames from incendiaries exploding nearby penetrated the building through the broken windows but were extinguished by the company's own fire brigade.

After World War II, IWC was forced to change its focus. All of Eastern Europe had fallen under the Iron Curtain, and the economy of Germany was in shambles. As a result, old contacts and connections with other countries in Europe and the Americas as well as Australia and the Far East were revived and intensified or established.

1970s - present

In the 1970s and 80s, the Swiss watchmaking industry underwent a phase of far-reaching technological change. Following in the wake of the use of miniaturized electric batteries as a source of energy for wristwatches from the late 1940s onwards and the invention of the transistor in 1947, purely mechanical watch technology developed into a hybrid discipline of precision mechanics and electronics.

The IWC Da Vinci

IWC managed to avoid investing heavily in expensive and eventually unsuccessful technologies, such as the electronically controlled balance. The UHRENFABRIK H. E. HOMBERGER co-founded and was a shareholder in the "Centre Électronique Horloger" (CEH) in Neuchâtel and was financially involved in the development of the Beta 21 quartz wristwatch movement, which was first presented to the public at the 1969 Industrial Fair in Basel. In actual value terms, this movement accounted for about 5-6% of total sales of quartz watches. Parallel to this, the company expanded its collection of jeweler watches to include ladies watches with mechanical movements. The year 1973 was IWC's most successful of the post-war period.

The cataclysmic rise in gold prices in 1974 had grave consequences for the watch exporting industry. Between 1970 and 1974 the price of gold rose from 4850 to 18 000 francs and the value of the dollar against the Swiss currency plummeted by up to 40%. As a result, the price of watch exports rose by as much as 250%. At the same time Japan was flooding the market with cheap quartz watches.

A change of direction was necessary and this led to the adoption of a number of measures. In order to survive, IWC, under the leadership of Director and CEO Otto Heller, built up a line of high-quality pocket watches, and, apart from setting up its own modern wristwatch and case manufacturing facilities, began working closely with Ferdinand A. Porsche as an external designer. In addition, IWC pioneered new watchmaking technologies, notably the first titanium bracelets, developed in 1978.

For its new plans IWC required a high level of venture capital. With the help of the Swiss Banking Corporation, the company was put in contact with VDO Adolf Schindling AG, which took a majority interest in IWC in 1978.

The IWC GST (Ref. 3707)

At the same time, IWC reacquired the name it had originally been given by its founder F.A. Jones (INTERNATIONAL WATCH CO. AG).

In 1981, Kawal Singh succeeded H.E. Homberger as general manager following the latter's retirement on age grounds. The new director, Günter Blümlein, pushed for rapid implementation of planned changes, put the existing advertising campaign to work, built up the customer base, and solidified IWC's finances.

In 1991 IWC director Günter Blümlein founded the LMH Group with its headquarters in Schaffhausen. With a 100% stake in IWC, 60% in Jaeger-LeCoultre and 90% in the Saxony-based watchmaking company of A. Lange & Söhne, the Group employed some 1440 persons.

In July 2000, LMH was acquired by Richemont, a Zug-based luxury goods group, for CHF 2.8 bn. Despite the takeover by Richemont, IWC was guaranteed that it would continue to be managed by the same executives from the LMH Group.

In the year 2001 IWC went online with the Collectors Forum.

Sales history

The company began keeping detailed records for every watch that has left the factory since 1885. Since 1885, details of the caliber, materials used and cases have been entered into the records. In the case of later models, these also include the reference number, delivery date and the name of the authorized dealer. For a small fee, the owner can obtain precise information about their watch, as long as the watch is at least ten years old.

The company claims that its service department has the parts and is capable of repairing and maintaining watches from every era since IWC's foundation in 1868."

IWC movements

Some modern movements in watches of IWC are based on movements supplied by ETA and heavily modified by IWC. This is common practice by many high end watch marques. In particular, the Caliber 30110 is a modified ETA 2892A2, and the Caliber 79230/79320/79350 is a modified ETA/Valjoux 7750. Like all high end automatic watches, IWC watches lose or gain approximately 4 seconds a day.

Movements not based on ETA movements include the Caliber 5000 and the Caliber 8000, which use the Pellaton winding system, and the pocket watch movements used in the Portuguese F.A. Jones and other IWC pocket watches. IWC also used a JLC meca-quartz movement in their older Portofino chronographs.

On-line auction

Since 1997, IWC has been offering a unique horological rarity for on-line auction annually organized at IWC's website. The proceeds from the auction are donated to the Ecole des Sables – Antoine de Saint Exupéry school in Mali. The school provides education for the Tuareg children.

The Big Pilot Saint Exupéry edition.

In 2007, the Company auctioned the platinum version of the Pilot's Watch Automatic Edition Antoine de Saint Exupéry, Reference 3201. The timepiece was created in tribute of the French author and aviation pioneer. The model was auctioned together with an original copy of Exupery's debut novel, *Courrier Sud* (*Southern Mail*), featuring a handwritten dedication by the author. In 2009 IWC introduced the Big Pilot edition Antoine de Saint Exupéry in 1900 pieces. Only one of them will be in platinum and will be auctioned for charity.

Publication

Four times a year, IWC publishes a customer magazine titled, *Watch International.* This publication is available in German, French and English, and includes stories, articles and features about IWC. "

The IWC Flagship Store in Hong Kong

External links

- Official IWC website [1]
- Information on IWC's engravings and motto [2]

Tissot

Tissot

Type	Member of the Swatch group
Industry	Watch manufacturing
Founded	1853 by Charles-Félicien Tissot and Charles-Emile Tissot
Headquarters	Le Locle, Switzerland
Number of locations	16,000
Area served	150 countries
Key people	François Thiébaud, (President) Georges Nicolas Hayek jun. (Chairmain of the Board)
Products	Wristwatches, pocket watches, timing devices/systems
Services	Timing systems
Employees	250
Parent	The Swatch Group Ltd.
Website	www.tissot.ch [1] www.t-touch.com [2]

Tissot is a Swiss watchmaker company founded in 1853 by Charles-Felicien Tissot and his son Charles-Emile who established the Tissot factory in the Swiss city of Le Locle, in the Neuchâtel area of the Jura Mountains.

Tissot should not be confused with Mathey-Tissot, a separate Swiss watchmaking firm established by Edmond Mathey-Tissot in 1886.

History

Tissot introduced the first mass-produced pocket watch and the first pocket watch with two times zones in 1853 and the first anti-magnetic watch in 1929-30. Charles-Emile Tissot left for Russia in 1858 and succeeded in selling their savonnette pocket watches across the Russian Empire. The Tissot company was also the first to make watches out of plastic (IDEA 2001 in 1971), stone (the Alpine granite Rock watch in 1985), mother of pearl (the Pearl watch in 1987), and wood (the Wood watch in 1988). Tissot merged with the Omega watch making family in 1930 and Tissot-Omega watches from this era are sought after by collectors.

Still based in Le Locle, Switzerland and present in more than 150 countries around the world, Tissot has been a member of The Swatch Group Ltd., the largest watch producer and distributor in the world, since 1983.

Tissot is an official timekeeper for the world championships in cycling, motorcycling, fencing and ice hockey, and was used for the Davis Cup in 1957 and Downhill Skiing in Switzerland in 1938. Tissot was also a key Sponsor for the Formula one teams Lotus, Renault and Sauber.

Tissot has become known in recent years for its tactile, or "T-Touch," technology; several new watches have touch-sensitive sapphire glasses and include compasses, barometers, altimeters and thermometers. T-Touch watches have been recently featured on Angelina Jolie's wrist in the movies *Lara Croft Tomb Raider: The Cradle of Life* and *Mr. & Mrs. Smith.*

Famous people who have worn Tissot watches include the actress Sarah Bernhardt, singer Carmen Miranda, Elvis Presley, Grace Kelly, and Nelson Mandela. James Stewart also wears a Tissot watch in the movie "Rear Window".

Sponsored people

- Nicky Hayden, American MotoGP Rider
- Danica Patrick, American Indycar Driver
- Michael Owen, English Footballer
- Barbie Hsu, Taiwanese Actress
- Deepika Padukone, Indian Actress
- Thomas Lüthi, Swiss 250cc Rider
- CBA Official Timekeeper
- IIHL Official Timekeeper
- NASCAR Official Timekeeper
- MotoGP Official Timekeeper
- AFL Official Timekeeper
- Asian Games Official Timekeeper

Watch models

- T-Touch Expert
- T-Touch
- T-Race MotoGP
- T-Race
- T-Navigator 3000
- T-Sport
- TXL & TXS
- PRS 516
- PRS 200
- PRC 200 Chronograph
- PRC 200
- PRC 100
- PR 50
- Bascule
- Six-T
- T-Wave
- Ice-T
- Equi-T
- Diver Seastar Automatic 1000
- Seastar 660
- Seastar 7
- Bellflhour
- Flower Power
- V8
- Cocktail
- Le Locle

- Heritage
- T-Lord
- Stylist BB

Tissot Le Locle

Tissot T-Touch

External links

- Official website [3]
- The Swatch Group [3]

Waltham Watch Company

Waltham Watch Company

Industry	Horology
Fate	Went out of business
Founded	1850
Defunct	1957/1994
Headquarters	Waltham, Massachusetts, United States
Products	Watches, Clocks & Aircraft Clocks
References: see Waltham International SA (Switzerland) & Waltham Aircraft Clock Corporation, Alabama (U.S.A.)	

The **Waltham Watch Company**, also known as the **American Waltham Watch Co.** and the **American Watch Co.**, produced about 40 million high quality watches, clocks, speedometers, compasses, time fuses and other precision instruments between 1850 and 1957.

WORKS OF THE AMERICAN WATCH COMPANY, WALTHAM, MASS.

History

In 1850, Roxbury, Massachusetts, David Davis, Edward Howard and Aaron Lufkin Dennison formed together the company that would later become the **Waltham Watch Company**. The revolutionary business plan was to manufacture the movement parts so precisely that they would become fully interchangeable. Based upon the experience of earlier failed trials, Howard and Dennison would eventually perfect and patent their precision watch making machines and create the *American System of Watch Manufacturing*.

American Horologe Company (Warren Manufacturing Company)

In 1851, according to some sources, the company took the name "American Horologe Company" and production started in the new factory building. However, in October 1886, Waltham co-founder, Aaron Lufkin Dennison, in a letter to author Crossman, refuted the name and stated that the first Company name was the Warren Manufacturing Company, named for General Warren of Roxbury, a famous soldier of the War of Independence.The word "watch" was specifically omitted to retain secrecy of the novel operation.

Late 1852, the first watches were complete. The first 17 watches, which ran for 8 days, marked "Howard, Davis & Dennison" were distributed among company officials. Number-1 given to Edward Howard resides in the Smithsonian Collection. Numbers 18 to 100 were named "Warren, Boston" and the following 800 "Samuel Curtis", after the financial backer. A few, marked "Fellows & Schell", sold for $40. January 1853 saw the introduction of the "P.S. Bartlett" watch(named for an early employee Patten Sargeant Bartlett).

Boston Watch Company

The company was renamed **Boston Watch Co.** in September 1853. A new factory was built in Waltham, Massachusetts, on the banks of the Charles River, which grew over the years to its present size. In October 1854 the company moved into the new factory. The next movements manufactured (1001-5000) were marked "Dennison, Howard, & Davis", "P.S.Bartlett", and "C.T. Parker". The company had financial difficulties and Edward Howard left to form E. Howard & Co..

Appleton Tracy & Company

Upon bankruptcy, the company was sold at auction to Royal E. Robbins, who reorganized it under the new name **Appleton Tracy & Co.** (ATCo) in May 1857. Bearing this name, the next movements produced, Waltham Model 1857 was the 1st pocket watch produced in America of standard parts. Serial numbers 5001 to 14,000. The "C.T. Parker" was introduced as the 1857 model. 399 units were made. Also 598 chronometers were manufactured.

American Watch Company

The **Waltham Improvement Co.** merged in January 1859 with the **Appleton, Tracy & Co.** forming the **American Watch Co.** (AWCo). In 1860, as President Abraham Lincoln was elected, the country was in Civil War. Production ground to a halt. However, the company decided to downsize to the lowest possible level to keep the factory open. It worked: Upon his Gettysburg Address, President Lincoln became the proud owner of a Waltham watch: Model 1857, grade "Wm. Ellery", serial number no 67613. A.W.Co. made unusual 14 size watch with "Push button" at 1 o'clock position to set the time. Serial No.2875426 Name: Bond St.

Waltham became the main supplier of Railroad chronometers to the various railroads in North America and in as many as 52 other countries of the world. In 1876, Waltham disclosed the first automatic screw making machinery and obtained the first Gold Medal in a watch precision contest at the Philadelphia Centennial Exposition. Not only the American Horology but also the world owes much to the early members of the Waltham Watch entity, such as Bacon, Church, Dennison, Fogg, H. Marsh, Webster and Woerd for their technical inventions and developments.

American Waltham Watch Company

In 1885, after 26 years, the company name changed to **American Waltham Watch Co.** (AWWCo) where it was to remain for the next 32 years. Most widely known under this name, the company would produce some of the finest examples of pocket watches ever created.

Magazine advertisement from 1913.

Waltham Watch Company

Two high-quality groups of watches were produced by Waltham as direct result of orders placed by the Canadian Pacific Railway. One large group has the shield and beaver emblem of the Railway engraved on the movements, and is known as the "CPR" type. The second group has "Canadian Railway Time Service" engraved on the movements, and is known as the "CRTS" type. They are both highly prized by collectors.

Waltham Precision Instruments Company

Waltham closed its factory doors and declared bankruptcy in 1949, alhtough the factory briefly reopened a few times (primarily to finish and case existing watch inventory for sale). Several different plans were presented to restart the business, but all failed for various reasons. In 1958, the company decided to get out of the consumer watch business completely, and reorganized into the Waltham Precision Instruments Company. All remaining watch inventory had been sold to the Hallmark Watch Company the previous year, and rights to the "Waltham" trademark were sold to a new Waltham Watch Company incorporated in Delaware in exchange for stock.

However, specialized clocks and chronographs for use in aircraft control panels continued to be made in the Waltham factory under the name of Waltham Precision Instruments Company until the company was sold in 1994. The company is now based in Alabama as the Waltham Aircraft Clock Corporation.

Waltham International SA Switzerland

The Waltham Watch Company went out of business in 1957, but had founded a subsidiary in Switzerland in 1954, Waltham International SA. Waltham International SA retains the right to the Waltham trade name outside of North America, and continues to produce mechanical wrist watches and mechanical pocket watches under the "Waltham" brand. It is a full-fledged member of the Federation of the Swiss Watch Industry FH.

Hallmark Watch Company

During their restructuring efforts in the 50's, Waltham opened an office in New York for the purposes of importing Swiss watch movements and cases. Due to restrictions placed on the company by their main creditor (the Restructuring Finance Corporation, they couldn't sell these watches directly, so they were sold through a independent company; the Hallmark Watch Company.

Waltham Watch Company (Delaware)

The Waltham Watch Company (later known as Waltham of Chicago) was founded by one of the executives of the Hallmark Watch Company to carry on the Waltham trade name in the watch business. In exchange for rights to the name, existing Waltham Watch Company (Mass) shareholders received 1 share of the new company for every 5 shares of the original company.

In 1959, the Waltham Watch Company merged with the Hallmark Watch Company, giving the new company access to replacement parts to service existing Waltham watch owners. Notwithstanding their efforts to present a seamless transition, the company came under much scrutiny by the FTC throughout the 60's, and ultimately was forced to change their advertising and branding policies to clearly indicate that they weren't directly related to the original Waltham company, and that their products were not made in America.

US & Canada Business

The United States & Canada businesses of Waltham are now owned by MZ Berger and Company manufacturing cheap watches in China for distribution solely in U.S.A. and Canada, outside of the watch industry dealerships.

Serial Numbers

Every watch movement was engraved with an individual serial number which can be used to estimate the date of production. Volunteers have created a database of Waltham serial numbers, models and grades, and descriptions of observed watches .

Abraham Lincoln's Watch

In tribute, upon the Gettysburg Address, he was presented with a **William Ellery**, key wind watch **Waltham Model 1857**, serial number **67613**. This watch is now in the collection of the National Museum of American History at the Smithsonian Institution in Washington, DC.

Waltham watch on the moon

Astronaut David Scott, commander of the Apollo 15 mission in 1971, wore a Waltham watch on his third lunar EVA when his standard Omega Speedmaster Professional chronograph became damaged. This was a Waltham branded Swiss made watch.

See also

- Elgin Watch Company
- Gruen Watch Co.
- Hamilton Watch Company
- Illinois Watch Company

References

- *Waltham Pocket Watch Guide*, by Roy Ehrhardt, First Edition Printed January 1976, ISBN 9-913902-17-9
- *The Complete Guide to American Pocket Watches*, by Cooksey Shugart, First Edition 1981, ISBN 0-517-543788
- *Complete Watch Guide*, by Cooksey Shugart, Tom Engle, Richard E. Gilbert, Edition 1998, ISBN 1-57432-064-5
- *Complete Guide to Watches*, by Tom Engle, Richard E. Gilbert, Cooksey Shugart, Twenty Seventh Edition, January 2007, ISBN 1-57432-553-1

- *Lincoln Collector: The Story of Oliver R. Barrett's Great Private Collection*, by Carl Sandburg, Bonanza Books, 1960
- *The Waltham Watch Company: A Case History*, by Vincent P. Carosso, Published by: The President and Fellows of Harvard College

External links

- Waltham Aircraft Clock Corporation [1].
- Waltham Serial Numbers [2]
- Extensive collection of Waltham watches [3]
- Charles River Museum of Industry [4]
- *Making Watches in Waltham*, 1867 **New York Times** article [5]
- NAWCC: National Association of Watch & Clocks Collectors [6],
- Waltham Pocket Watch Company [7]
- Boston The Cradle of American Watchmaking [8]
- The Boston Watch Co [9]
- Origins of Waltham Model 57 [10]
- Time Museum Rockford, Illinois, U.S.A. [11]
- Philadelphia Exhibition 1876 Report to the Federal High Council by Ed. Favre-Perret (1877) [12]
- American and Swiss Watchmaking in 1876 by Jacques David [13]
- The Watch Factories of America Past and Present by Henry G. Abbott (1888) [14]
- Watchmaking and the American System of Manufacturing (2009) [15]

Waltham International

Waltham International

Waltham International SA was founded in 1954 in Lausanne, Switzerland, by the American Waltham Watch Company, Waltham, Massachusetts, to provide the necessary watch and movement parts, which were not readily available in U.S.A.

Now located in Marin-Epagnier/Neuchâtel, Switzerland, Waltham International SA manufacture Waltham luxury Swiss watches, furthering the spirit of excellence of the 1850 Waltham founders, since the U.S. parent company 1957 discontinued production of watches for the consumer market. Waltham's main market is Japan, through its distributor Heiwado & Co.

(Production of specialized clocks for aircraft continued in the original US factory until the parent company was finally sold in 1994. The new owners kept the Waltham name, but moved production to Ozark, Alabama, see Waltham Aircraft Clock Corporation.)

External links

- Waltham Serial Numbers [1]
- Waltham International SA [2]

External links About the History of Waltham

- Boston The Cradle of American Watchmaking [8]
- The Boston Watch Co [9]
- Origins of Waltham Model 57 [10]
- Time Museum Rockford, Illinois, U.S.A. [11]
- Philadelphia Exhibition 1876 Report to the Federal High Council by Ed. Favre-Perret (1877) [12]
- American and Swiss Watchmaking in 1876 by Jacques David [13]
- The Watch Factories of America Past and Present by Henry G. Abbott (1888) [14]
- Watchmaking and the American System of Manufacturing (2009) [15]

Breitling

Breitling

Breitling is a brand of Swiss watches from Grenchen, Canton of Solothurn (originally founded in Saint-Imier, Bernese Jura by Léon Breitling in 1884). The watchmaker offers Certified Chronometers designed primarily for aviation use, though most frequently worn as high-end luxury watches. Breitling's watches offer aviation functions, though their chronograph functions have become more of status symbols than practically applied tools. They typically have a large face (e.g. the *Breitling for Bentley Motors* edition has a 48 mm Case Diameter) for better visibility and to allow display of more information on the analog dials. Many models feature an automatic winding mechanism that is purely mechanical (i.e. using no electronic components). Many Breitling watches are equipped with additional functions such as the flyback function, split-second, moon phase, date display and other complications.

All Breitling watches are manufactured in Switzerland and are made from Swiss components. Raw movements are obtained from ETA and Valjoux and are modified in the Breitling Chronometrie Workshops, before undergoing COSC (Contrôle Officiel Suisse des Chronomètres) certification. As of 2009, Breitling now makes a manufacture movement, designed, manufactured and assembled completed in-house (B01 Calibre). [1]

Quartz models such as the *Breitling Aeromarine Colt* start at $2,055.00 on a rubber strap, while typical prices of mechanical, steel cased models are $7,300 (US) for the *Breitling for Bentley Motors* model. The expense is due to the exclusivity of the Bentley trademark, as well as the 38 jewel self-winding movement as these steel cased models are more expensive than some of Breitling's Titanium or Gold models. Some special edition models also include diamonds on various parts of the watch. I.E. Diamond Bezel, Diamond Bracelet, etc.

Breitling was a sponsor of Team Bentley during their Le Mans 24 Hours campaign, running from 2001-2003. To commemorate this event, Breitling created the Limited Edition Breitling Bentley 24 Le Mans Watch [2].

The Breitling Navitimer

Breitling Navitimer wristwatch with circular slide rule.

In the 1940s, Breitling added a circular slide rule to the bezel of their chronograph models for use by aircraft pilots. This became the famous *Navitimer* model. During the 1950s and 1960s, a version of the Navitimer was offered by the Aircraft Owners and Pilots Association with the AOPA logo on the dial.

In 1961, Scott Carpenter, one of the original astronauts in the Mercury space program, approached Breitling with idea of incorporating a 24 hour dial instead of the normal 12 hour dial. This was needed because of the lack of day and night during space travel. Breitling complied, and produced the 24 hour Navitimer which Carpenter wore on his 1962 space flight. Breitling then proceeded to produce the 24 hour version as the so-called *Cosmonaute* Navitimer - under both Breitling and AOPA logos.

The Breitling Emergency

Breitling Emergency

The *Breitling Emergency* version contains a radio transmitter for civil aviation use which broadcasts on the 121.5 MHz distress frequency and serves as a back-up for ELT-type airborne beacons. (For military users, Breitling has equipped the *Emergency* with a miniaturized transmitter operating on the 243.0 MHz military frequency.) Under normal conditions—flat terrain or calm seas—the signal can be picked up at a range of up to 90 nautical miles (167 km) by search aircraft flying at 20,000 feet (6,000 m). As of 1 February 2009, the Cospas-Sarsat Satellite System will no longer monitor the 121.5/243.0 MHz frequency; however, the signal transmitted by the *Emergency* was never strong enough to be picked up by satellite, and Breitling has announced that, as these frequencies will still be monitored by aviation, particularly during the localization phase of a rescue attempt, there are no plans to modify the signal's frequency.[3]

Reuters reported that two British pilots, Squadron Leader Steve Brooks and Flight Lieutenant Hugh Quentin-Smith, crashed their helicopter in Antarctica and were rescued after activating their Breitling Emergency transmitter watches. The two pilots were in their lifeboat when a Chilean Otter aircraft found them after homing in on signals from their watches. [4]

The *Emergency* is available for customers who do not hold a pilot's licence, but they must sign an agreement stating that they will bear the full costs of a rescue intervention should they trigger the distress beacon. The model was heavily advertised by the *Breitling Orbiter 3*—both Brian Jones and Bertrand Piccard were wearing the *Emergency*. Also, Bear Grylls wears an *Emergency* with yellow face and rubber strap in many episodes of Man vs. Wild.

Additional Breitling Models

Breitling Navitimer

Breitling for Bentley Motors: Features a 30 second chronograph

Breitling Super Avenger (48 mm)

Breitling Super Avenger (48 mm)

Base Movements

Breitling base Movements

Breitling Movement	Base Movement
B01	Calibre Breitling, first and only in-house movement
B10	ETA 2892-A2
B11	Lemania 1873
B12	Lemania 187
B13	Valjoux 7750

B17	ETA 2824
B18	ETA 2892-A2
B19	ETA 2892-A2
B20	Valjoux 7750
B22	ETA 2892-A2
B24	Valjoux 7754
B26	ETA 2892-A2
B30	ETA 2892-A2
B33	ETA 2892-A2
B34	ETA 1185/86
B35	ETA 2892
B36	ETA 2892
B38	ETA 2892-A2
B39	ETA 2892-A2
B40	ETA 2892-A2
B41	ETA 2892
B42	ETA 2892
B43	Valjoux 7758
B44	ETA 2892
B45	ETA 2834-2

External links

- Breitling home page [5] (requires Adobe Flash Player)
- Guide to the Breitling Navitimer [6]
- Breitling information [7]

Omega SA

Omega SA

OMEGA	
Type	Private (subsidiary of the Swatch Group)
Industry	Watch manufacturing
Founded	1848
Founder(s)	Louis Brandt
Headquarters	Bienne, Switzerland
Key people	Nicolas G. Hayek, Chairman Stephen Urquhart, President
Products	Watches
Parent	The Swatch Group
Website	omegawatches.com [1]

Omega SA is a Swiss luxury watchmaker based in Biel/Bienne, Switzerland. Omega is one of the most known and recognized watches in the world. Omega watch was the choice of NASA and the first watch on the Moon in 1969. Omega was the official Time Keeping device of the 2010 Vancouver Winter Olympics. James Bond has worn it in films since 1995; other famous Omega wearers are John F. Kennedy , Prince William, Buzz Aldrin, Joe Biden, George Clooney, Nicole Kidman, Michael Phelps, Zhang Ziyi and Cindy Crawford. Omega estimates that 7 out of every 10 people have heard of Omega watches. Omega is owned by the Swatch Group.

History

Foundation

The forerunner of Omega was founded at La Chaux-de-Fonds, Switzerland in 1848 by 23-year-old Louis Brandt, who assembled key-wound precision pocket watches from parts supplied by local craftsmen. He sold his watches from Italy to Scandinavia by way of England, his chief market. After Louis Brandt's death in 1879, his two sons Louis-Paul and César, troubled by irregular deliveries of questionable quality, abandoned the unsatisfactory assembly workshop system in favour of in-house manufacturing and total production control.

The workbench of Louis Brandt with a photograph of the founder.

Relocation

Due to the greater supply of manpower, communications and energy in Biel/Bienne, the enterprise moved into a small factory in January 1880, then bought the entire building in December. Two years later the company moved into a converted spinning-factory in the Gurzelen area of Biel/Bienne, where its headquarters are still situated today.

Their first series-produced calibres, Labrador and Gurzelen, as well as the famous *Omega* calibre of 1894, would ensure the brand's marketing success.

Omega medical chronograph with outer pulsations track, ca. 1950

Merger

Louis-Paul and César Brandt both died in 1903, leaving one of Switzerland's largest watch companies — with 240,000 watches produced annually and employing 800 people — in the hands of four young people, the oldest of whom, Paul-Emile Brandt, was not yet 24.

Brandt was the great architect and builder of Omega. His influence would be felt over the next half-century. The economic difficulties brought on by the First World War would lead him to work actively from 1925 toward the union of Omega and Tissot, then to their merger in 1930 into the group SSIH, Geneva.

Omega Seamaster De Ville, an early "waterproof" watch, with automatic movement and date, in 14k gold

Financial takeover

Weakened by the severe monetary crisis and recession of 1975 to 1980, SSIH was bailed out by the banks in 1981. During this period, Seiko expressed interest in acquiring Omega, but nothing came out of the talks.

Switzerland's other watch making giant Allgemeine Schweizerische Uhrenindustrie AG (ASUAG - supplier of a large range of Swiss movements and watch assemblers) was in economic difficulty. It was the principal manufacturer of *Ébauche* (unfinished movements) and owner, through their sub-holding company GWC (General Watch Co), of various other Swiss watch brands including Longines, Rado, Certina and Mido.

After drastic financial restructuring, the R&D departments of ASUAG and SSIH merged production operations at the ETA complex in Granges. The two companies completely merged forming ASUAG-SSIH, a holding company, in 1983.

Two years later this holding company was taken over by a group of private investors led by Nicolas Hayek. Renamed SMH, Société de Microélectronique et d'Horlogerie, this new group over the next decade proceded to become one of the top watch producers in the world. In 1998 it became the Swatch Group, which now manufactures Omega and other brands such as Blancpain, Swatch, and Breguet.

Movements and the co-axial escapement

In 1999, with the successful own development of Calibre 2500, Omega made history by introducing the first mass-produced watch incorporating the co-axial escapement — invented by English watchmaker George Daniels. Considered by many to be one of the more significant horological advances since the invention of the lever escapement, the co-axial escapement functions with virtually no lubrication, thereby eliminating one of the shortcomings of the traditional lever escapement. Through using radial friction instead of sliding friction at the impulse surfaces the co-axial escapement significantly reduces friction, theoretically resulting in longer service intervals and greater accuracy over time.

On January 24, 2007 Omega unveiled its new Calibres 8500 and 8501, two co-axial (25,200 bph) movements created exclusively from inception by Omega.

Omega watches in space exploration

Main article: Omega Speedmaster Professional

The Omega Speedmaster, or "Moonwatch", selected by NASA for all the Apollo missions

The selection of the "Omega Speedmaster Professional Chronograph" for American astronauts was the subject of a rivalry between Omega and Bulova.

All subsequent manned NASA missions also used this handwound wristwatch. NASA started selecting the chronograph in the early 60s and automatic chronograph wristwatches were not available until 1969.

First watch on the moon

The "Omega Speedmaster Professional Chronograph" was the first watch on the Moon, worn by "Buzz" Aldrin. This watch is now believed lost. Aldrin mentions in his book *Return to Earth* that when donating several items to the Smithsonian Institution, his Omega was one of the few things that was stolen from his personal effects.

In 2007, to mark the 50th anniversary of the Omega Speedmaster Professional Chronograph, the Omega company unveiled the commemorative *Speedmaster Professional Chronograph Moonwatch.* The watch had the distinctive features of the first hand-winding Omega Speedmaster introduced in 1957. It was sold in an edition of 5,957.

Copyright Lawsuit

Omega is currently in a lawsuit against wholesaler Costco over grey market imports of Omega watches that challenges the legality of the first-sale doctrine with regards to international imports, Omega v. Costco. This lawsuit has been granted certiorari by the Supreme Court of the United States.

Sponsorship, product placement, advertising, and sport

James Bond

Omega has been associated with James Bond movies since 1995. That year, Pierce Brosnan took over the role of James Bond and began wearing the Omega Seamaster Quartz Professional (model 2541.80.00) in the movie *GoldenEye.* In all later films, Brosnan wore an Omega Seamaster Professional Chronometer (model 2531.80.00). The producers wanted to update the image of the fictional "super-spy" to a more distinctly sophisticated "Euro" look.

The Omega Seamaster, a deep diving watch. The second crown (at 10 o'clock) is a helium release valve to allow helium out of the watch after diving at great depth. The watch is similar to that shown in recent James Bond films, in which this valve is transformed into improbable hidden gadgets.

Another possible reason for the change from the Rolex Submariner that Bond had previously worn was a change in the business environment surrounding modern high-profile films and product placement. Omega was eager to participate in high profile co-promotions/product placement opportunities, especially the James Bond franchise, to further its brand image/awareness. It accomplished this by supplying products and finance (something that the conservative Rolex company avoids, presumably because it sees no benefit for itself).

For the 40th anniversary of James Bond (2002) a commemorative edition of the watch was made available model 2537.80.00 (10,007 units). The watch is identical to the model 2531.80.00 except the blue watch dial had a 007 logo inscribed across it and also machined into the caseback. The band also had 007 inscribed on the clasp.

Daniel Craig, the current James Bond of *Casino Royale,* and *Quantum of Solace* also wears the Omega Seamaster: the Seamaster Planet Ocean (model 2900.50.91) in the first part Casino Royale, and in the latter part (from travelling to Montenegro), and even goes so far as to mention Omega by name when questioned by Vesper Lynd. In connection with the launch of the film, Omega released an 007-special of the Professional 300M, featuring the 007-gun logo on the second hand and the rifle pattern on the watch face, this being a stylized representation of the gunbarrel sequence of Bond movies.

Omega released a second James Bond limited edition watch in 2006. This was a *Seamaster Planet Ocean* model with a limited production of 5007 units. The model is similar to what Craig wears earlier on in the film; however, it has a small orange colored 007 logo on the second hand, an engraved caseback signifying the Bond connection, and an engraved 007 on the clasp. In the newest movie, Quantum of Solace, Craig wears the Omega Seamaster Planet Ocean with a black face and steel braclet (42 mm version). Another limited edition was released featuring the checkered "PPK grip" face with the Quantum of Solace logo over it.

Sports sponsorship

Omega has frequently been the official timekeeper for the Olympics, beginning with the 1932 Summer Olympics. It was the official timekeeper for the 2006 Winter Olympics and for the 2008 Summer Olympics, and did the same for the 2010 Winter Olympics. For the 2008 Olympics, Omega brought out an Olympic edition with its logo on the second hand. Olympic swimmer and multiple gold medalist Michael Phelps is an Omega Ambassador and wears the Seamaster Planet Ocean.

Providing support to Emirates Team New Zealand and representing the team's official watch, in 2007 Omega introduced the Seamaster NZL-32 chronograph, with the name suggested by the name of the boat that won the America's Cup in 1995. The watch was developed in cooperation with Dean Barker, skipper of Team New Zealand and Omega Ambassador.

Omega also sponsored a number of golf tournaments.

Watch models

For men

- Constellation [2]
- Omega Seamaster
  - includes the Planet Ocean, Ploprof, Aqua Terra, and Seamaster Bond Styles
- Speedmaster [3]
  - includes the famous Omega Speedmaster Professional Moon watch

The Seamaster Planet Ocean 600 M diving watch is currently Omega's newest version of the Seamaster Series.

- Deville [4]
- Specialities [5]
  - includes their skeleton Seamaster and Central Tourbillon DeVille.

For women

- Constellation [6]
- Seamaster [7]
- Speedmaster [8]
- Deville [9]
- Specialities [10]

See also

- Société de Microélectronique et d'Horlogerie
- Joseph Reiser
- Ernst Thomke
- Nicolas G. Hayek

External links

- Official website [11]

TAG Heuer

TAG Heuer

Type	Member of the LVMH group
Industry	Watch manufacturing
Founded	1860 by Edouard Heuer
Headquarters	La Chaux-de-Fonds, Switzerland
Key people	Jean-Christophe Babin, President & CEO Jack W. Heuer, Honorary President
Products	Wristwatches, timing devices/systems, fashion accessories, eyewear
Parent	LVMH Moët Hennessy Louis Vuitton S.A.
Website	TAGHeuer.com [1]

History

Nineteenth century

The TAG Heuer company has its roots in 1860 when Edouard Heuer founded a watchmaking company in St-Imier, Switzerland, patenting his first chronograph in 1882. In 1887 Heuer patented an 'oscillating pinion' still used by major watchmakers for mechanical chronographs.

Early twentieth century

In 1911, Heuer received a patent for the "Time of Trip", the first dashboard chronograph. Designed for use in automobiles and aircraft, two large hands mounted from the center pinion indicate the time of day, as on a traditional clock. A small pair of hands, mounted at the top of the dial (12 o'clock position) indicates the duration of the trip (up to 12 hours). A top-mounted crown allows the user to set the time; a button mounted in that crown operates the start / stop / reset functions of the "duration of trip" counter.

Heuer introduced its first wrist chronograph in 1914. The crown was at the twelve o'clock position, as these first wrist chronographs were adapted from pocket chronographs. In 1916, Heuer introduced the "Micrograph", the first stopwatch accurate to 1/100th of a second. This model was soon followed by the "Semikrograph", a stopwatch that offered 1/50th of a second timing, as well as a split-second function (which allows the user to determine the interval between two contestants or events).

Timepieces of the 1930s and 1940s

In 1933, Heuer introduced the "Autavia", a dashboard timer used for automobiles and aviation (whence its name, from "AUTos" and "AVIAtion"). The companion "Hervue" was a clock that could run for eight days without being wound. Over the period from 1935 through the early 1940s, Heuer manufactured chronographs for pilots in the German air force, known as "Flieger" (pilots) chronographs. The earlier version featured a hinged-back case and one pusher (for start / stop / reset); the later version had a snap-back case and added a second pusher (for time-in and time-out). All these Flieger chronographs had two-registers, with a capacity of 30 minutes.".

In the mid-1940s, Heuer expanded its line of chronographs to include both two and three register models, as well as a three-register chronograph that included a full calendar function (day / date / month). As the highest development of Heuer's chronographs, these "triple calendar" chronographs were offered in stainless steel, 14 carat gold 18 and 22 carat gold cases. Dial colors were white, black or copper.

1950s Chronographs

In the early 1950s, Heuer produced watches for the American retailer Abercrombie & Fitch. The "Seafarer" and "Auto-Graph" were unique chronographs produced by Heuer to be sold by Abercrombie & Fitch. The "Seafarers" had special dials—with blue, green and yellow patterns—that showed the high and low tides. This dial could also be used to track the phases of the moon. Heuer produced a version of the "Seafarer" for sale under the Heuer name, with this model called the "Mareographe". The "Auto-Graph" was produced in 1953 and 1954, and featured a tachymeter scale on the dial and a hand that could be preset to a specific point on the scale. This allowed a rally driver or navigator to determine whether the car was achieving the desired pace, over a measured mile. Advertisements and literature also pointed out that this hand could be rotated to count golf scores or other events.

Late 1950s -- New Series of Dashboard Timers

From as early as 1911, Heuer had manufactured timepieces to be mounted on the dashboards of automobiles, aircraft and boats. These clocks and timers included a variety of models, designed to address specific needs of racers and rallyists. In 1958, Heuer introduced a new line of dashboard timepieces, which included the Master Time (eight-day clock), the Monte Carlo (12-hour stopwatch), the Super Autavia (full chronograph), Sebring (60-minute, split second timer) and Auto-Rallye

(60-minute stopwatch). Heuer continued to manufacture these dashboard timepieces into the 1980s, at which time they were discontinued. Heuer also introduced timing devices for ski and motor racing events, including the prestigious Formula One.

1960s Chronographs

From the 1950s to the 1970s, Heuers were popular watches among automobile racers, both professionals and amateurs. Heuer was a leading producer of stopwatches and timing equipment, based on the volume of its sales, so it was only natural that racers, their crews and event sponsors began to wear Heuer's chronographs. Special versions of Heuer chronographs were produced with logos of the Indianapolis Motor Speedway, as well as the names or logos of racing teams or sponsors (for example, Shelby Cobra, MG and Champion Sparkplugs).

Autavia, 1962

In 1962, Heuer became the first Swiss watchmaker in space. John Glenn wore a Heuer stopwatch when he piloted the Mercury Atlas 6 spacecraft on the first US manned space flight to orbit the earth. This stopwatch was the back-up clock for the mission and was started manually by Glenn 20 seconds into the flight. It is currently on display at the San Diego Air and Space Museum.

Carrera, 1963

The Autavia chronograph was introduced in 1962 and featured a rotating bezel, marked in either hours, minutes, decimal minutes (1/100th minute increments) or with a tachymeter scale. All manual-wind Autavias from the 1960s had a black dial, with white registers. Early cases had a screw-back and later models (from and after 1968) had snap-backs. The "Autavia" name had previously been used on Heuer's dashboard timers (described above).

The Carrera chronograph, designed by Jack Heuer, was introduced in 1963. The Carrera had a very simple design, with only the registers and applied markers on the dial. The fixed inner bezel is divided into 1/5 second increments. The 1960s Carreras were available with a variety of dials, including all-white, all-black, white registers on a black dial, and black registers on a black dial. A three-register, triple calendar version of the Carrera was introduced around 1968.

Most of Heuer chronographs from this period—including the Autavias and Carreras—used movements manufactured by Valjoux, including the Valjoux 72 movement (for a 12-hour chronograph) and the Valjoux 92 movement (for a 30-minute or 45-minute chronograph). The Valjoux 72 movement utilized a 'tri-compax' design, with three registers on the dial—one register for the chronograph hours (at the bottom), one register for the chronograph minutes (at the right), and a third register for a continuously running second hand (at the left). The second hand for the chronograph was mounted on the center pinion, along with the time-of-day hands.

Heuer acquired the "Leonidas" brand in the early 1960s, with the combined company marketing watches under the "Heuer-Leonidas" name. One of the designs that Heuer acquired from Leonidas was the "Bundeswehr" chronograph, used by the German air force. These "BWs" feature a 'fly-back' mechanism, so that when the chronograph is reset to zero, it immediately begins running again, to time the next segment or event.

World's First Automatic Chronographs

Commencing in the mid-1960s, Heuer was part of a partnership (with Breitling and Hamilton) that sought to introduce the world's first automatic chronograph. Seiko (a Japanese watch manufacturer) and Zenith (a Swiss watch manufacturer) were also seeking to be the first to offer these chronographs. These projects were conducted in secret, as none of the competitors wanted the other companies to be aware of their efforts. Most agree that the Heuer-Breitling venture was first to introduce their new line of automatic chronographs, with Heuer-Breitling-Hamilton holding lavish press conferences in Geneva and New York, on March 3, 1969, to show their new lines of chronographs.

Heuer's first automatic chronographs were the Autavia, Carrera and Monaco. These were powered by the Cal 11 and Cal 12 movements (12-hour chronograph); Cal 14 movement (12-hour chronograph and additional hand for GMT / second time-zone) and the Cal 15 movement (30-minute chronograph). Unusually, the winding crown was on the left, with the pushers for the chronograph on the right. The earliest of Heuer's Cal 11 chronographs (from 1969) were named "Chrono-Matic". In the early 1970s, Heuer expanded its line of automatic chronographs to include the Daytona, Montreal, Silverstone, Calculator, Monza and Jarama models, all of them powered by the Caliber 11 movement.

The Heuer Monaco 40th Anniversary re-edition with Calibre 11, is a limited edition contemporary replica of the original Monaco.

Several of the automatic Heuer chronographs powered by the Caliber 11 series of movements are associated with automobile racing and specific drivers. Steve McQueen wore a blue Monaco in the 1971 movie, *Le Mans* (with this model now referred to as the "McQueen Monaco") and Swiss Formula One star Jo Siffert customarily wore a white-dialed Autavia with black registers. In 1974, Heuer produced a special version of the black-dialed Autavia that was offered by the Viceroy cigarette company, in a special promotion for $88. The Viceroy advertisements for this promotion featured racer Parnelli Jones, this version of the Autavia got to be called the "Viceroy".

Chronographs of the 1970s and 1980s

In 1975, Heuer introduced the Chronosplit, a digital chronograph with dual LED and LCD displays. Later versions featured two LCD displays.

Heuer began using the Valjoux 7750 movement in its automatic chronographs, with the Kentucky and Pasadena models (both introduced in 1977). The Valjoux 7750 movement was a three-register chronograph (with seconds, minutes and hours), that also offered day / date windows.

In the mid-1970s, Heuer introduced a series of chronographs powered by the Lemania 5100 movement. The Lemania 5100 movements have the minute hand for the chronograph on the center pinion (rather than on a smaller register), greatly improving legibility. The Lemania 5100 movement is considered very rugged and has been used in a variety of chronographs issued to military pilots. There are ten models of Heuer chronographs powered by the Lemania 5100—Reference 510.500 (stainless steel), 510.501 (black coated), 510.502 (olive drab coated), 510.503 (pewter coated), 510.511 (Carrera dialed acrylic crystal PVD finish), 510.523 (Carrera dialed acrylic crystal stainless steel), as well as models with the names Silverstone (steel case with black dial) and Cortina (steel case with blue dial); the Reference 510.543 was made for the A.M.I. (Italian Air Force) and a special edition (with no reference number marked on the case) was made for AudiSport.

Formation

TAG Heuer was formed in 1985 when TAG (Techniques d'Avant Garde), manufacturers of high-tech items such as ceramic turbochargers for Formula One cars, acquired Heuer.

On September 13, 1999 TAG Heuer accepted a bid from LVMH Moët Hennessy Louis Vuitton S.A. of SwFr1.15 billion (£452.15 million) (US$739 million) contingent upon a transfer of 50.1% of stocks.

Current models

TAG Heuer is known for producing luxury timepieces.

The lines include Formula One, Aquaracer, Link, Carrera, Monaco and Grand Carrera.

A TAG Heuer Grand Carrera RS.

Tag Heuer, in keeping with its image as a luxury brand with an innovative spirit, has long standing links with the world of sport and Hollywood. Tag Heuer has been the official timekeeper of the three Summer Olympic Games of the 1920s, the Skiing World Championships, the Formula One World Championships and having developed a watch for the McLaren F1 team. The brand has also had a long list of sports and Hollywood ambassadors.

Some of the more recently announced models include the Monaco V4 (the movement of which is driven by belts rather than gears); the Carrera Calibre 360 (the first mechanical wrist chronograph to measure and display time to 1/100th of a second) and the Monaco 69 (with both a digital chronograph accurate to a millisecond and a traditional mechanical movement, with a hinged mechanism allowing wearers to flip the watch between its two separate dials).

Awards

In 2007 TAG Heuer won the iF product design award for its Monaco Calibre 360 LS Concept Chronograph. The award was given away by the International Forum Design Hannover GmbH, held in Hanover, Germany. The watch received the prestigious award in the Leisure/Lifestyle category. It was chosen among more than 2,200 timepieces presented by watchmakers from 35 countries. TAG Heuer received the iF product design award for the second time in two years. In 2006 another TAG Heuer watch, entitled Professional Golf Watch, won in the same Leisure/Lifestyle category. The design of the Professional Golf Watch was developed with Tiger Woods.

External links

- Official website [2]

Patek Philippe & Co.

Patek Philippe & Co.

Type	Private
Industry	Watch Making
Founded	1851
Headquarters	Geneva, Switzerland
Area served	Worldwide
Products	Watches
Revenue	5.5 Billion Dollars
Website	www.patek.com [1]

Patek Philippe & Co. (PP) is a Swiss luxury watch *manufacture* located in Geneva and the Vallée de Joux. Considered by some watch enthusiasts as one of the best traditional watch companies in the world. Other companies include Vacheron Constantin and Audemars Piguet which is considered as three kings of *haute horlogerie*. There are only a handful potential contender such as A. Lange & Söhne, Breguet, Blancpain, Glashütte Original, Jaeger-LeCoultre, Ulysse Nardin and Zenith (watchmaker).

History

Amongst manufacturers, PP has a long history. Polish watchmaker Antoni Patek started making pocket watches in 1839 in Geneva, along with his fellow Polish migrant Franciszek Czapek. They separated in 1844, and in 1845 Patek joined with the French watchmaker Adrien Philippe, inventor of the keyless winding mechanism. In 1851, Patek Philippe & Co was founded.

In 1868, Patek Philippe made their first wrist-watch. They have also pioneered the perpetual calendar, split-seconds hand, chronograph, and minute repeater in watches.

The company, like other Swiss manufacturers, produces mostly mechanical movements of the automatic and manual wind variety, but has produced quartz watches in the past and even a digital wrist watch, the Ref. 3414. PP is notable for manufacturing its own watch components.

Patek Philippe timepieces have recorded high closing prices in auctions worldwide. A large part of the demand for auction pieces is driven by Patek Philippe themselves, as they are often purchasing in the auction market to add to the collection of the Patek Philippe Museum in Geneva.

The company is currently owned by the Stern family, led by Philippe Stern and his son Thierry Stern.

Notable watches

Most expensive

Patek Philippe produced an ultra-complicated (with 24 functions) pocket-watch for Henry Graves, Jr., who entered into a friendly horological competition with James Ward Packard, which resulted in the production of the watch (known as "The Supercomplication") sold to Mr. Graves in 1933. After his death, the watch was auctioned at Sotheby's in December 1999 for USD$11,000,000, at that time the most expensive timepiece ever sold. On April 10, 2008, "Ref. 5002P Sky Moon Tourbillon" a platinum Patek Philippe tourbillon wristwatch made the world record as the most expensive modern wristwatch sold at Hong Kong Sotheby's for HK$11.75 million ($1.49 million US). The previous record was held by a Vacheron Constantin *Tour de l'Ile* wristwatch, which sold at Antiquorum for $1.4 million in Geneva in 2005. On May 10, 2010, Patek Philippe beat its own record: the most expensive wristwatch in history was sold at an auction by Christie's in Geneva for 6.26 million swiss francs ($5.50 million US), purchased by a Swiss Privatemuseum. The historically valuable Patek Philippe chronograph wristwatch, from yellow gold has a perpetual calendar and moonphase display, and was produced in 1943 in the Geneva manufacture of Patek Philippe. Christie's estimated the value of about 1,5 (1.31$) – 2,5 (2.19$) million Swiss francs.

Watches owned by royalty

Patek Philippe watches have enjoyed great demand among discerning collectors and watch connoisseurs of a high social status and wealth. Since Queen Victoria's reign, monarchs, popes, political leaders, and rulers have purchased timepieces manufactured by the brand either for their personal use or as a precious gift to be presented to an important guest, or in recognition of someone's remarkable bravery and loyalty.

In 1851, Patek Philippe started supplying its watches to Queen Victoria and her consort, Prince Albert. Timepieces of the Genevan manufacturer immediately attracted attention of all the royal courts of Europe. Queen Victoria acquired a key-wound Patek Philippe watch created in a pendant style in November 1851 during the Great Exhibition of London. Queen Victoria owned one more exclusive Patek Philippe timepiece to be worn pinned to clothing. This watch was suspended from a diamond and enamel brooch.

The list of Patek Philippe notable past clientele also highlights Pope Pius IX, Pope Leo XIII, Christian IX and Louise (the king and queen of Denmark), Victor-Emanuel III (king of Italy and Duke of Savoy),

Hussein Kamel (Sultan of Egypt from 1914 to 1918)

Anniversary edition

In 1989, Patek created one of the most complicated mechanical watches ever made, the *Calibre 89*, created for the 150th anniversary of the company. It holds 39 complications, including the date of Easter, time of sunrise, equation of time, sidereal time, and many other indicators. 1,728 unique parts allow sidereal time a 2,800 star chart, and more. The Calibre 89 is also able to add a day to February for leap years while leaving out the extra day for every 100 year interval.

Lever escapement

In 2005 the company introduced the Silicon escapement wheel to the industry.

Gallery

Combined chronograph and calendar/moonphase wristwatch

Calendar and moonphase pocket-watch

Chronograph

Calendar and moonphase wristwatch

Watch from 1940s, Ref. 1543

Inside watch, Ref. 1543

Circa 1999 men's quartz Calatrava in yellow gold, with second hand and date

See also

- Calatrava (watch)
- Automatic watch
- Franciszek Czapek
- List of watch manufactures

External links

- Patek Philippe Official Site [2]
- Factory Tour and Watch Company Comparison [3]
- An article about Patek Philippe's watches [4]

Vacheron Constantin

Vacheron Constantin

Type	Member of the Richemont Group
Industry	Watch manufacturing
Founded	1755 by Jean-Marc Vacheron
Headquarters	Geneva, Switzerland
Key people	Jean-Marc Vacheron and François Constantin, founders
Products	Prestige watches
Website	[1] [1]

Vacheron Constantin is a Swiss *manufacture* of prestige watches and a brand of the Richemont group. Considered by the watches enthusiast as the best traditional watch maker in the world along with Patek Philippe & Co..

It employs around 400 people worldwide, most of whom are based in the manufacturing plant; a modern building in Geneva. The brand is sold in almost 80 countries around the world, distributed through 15 boutiques that sell no other brand, and over 500 points of sale.

Previous Vacheron Constantin owners include Napoleon Bonaparte, Pope Pius XI, the Duke of Windsor and Harry Truman.

History

Vacheron Constantin was founded in Geneva, Switzerland in 1755 by Jean-Marc Vacheron. This makes it the oldest watch manufacturer in the world with an uninterrupted history. Besides being a young businessman, Vacheron was also a talented craftsman. In 1770 his company created the first complication, and nine years later he designed the first engine-turned dials.

The son of Jean-Marc Vacheron, Abraham, took over the family business in 1785. During this period the company was able to survive the French Revolution (1789–1799). Later, in 1810, Jaques-Barthélemy Vacheron, the grandson of the founder, becomes the head of the company. He was the first to initiate the company's exports to France and Italy.

Later, Jaques-Barthélemy realized that he was not able to handle his business alone. In order to travel overseas and sell the company's products, he needed a partner. Consequently, in 1819 François Constantin became the associate of Vacheron. The company continued its activity under the name "Vacheron & Constantin".

François Constantin traveled around the world and marketed watches. Thus he helped the company to open new markets. The main market was North America. The company's motto (which remains today), "Do better if possible and that is always possible", first appeared in Constantin's letter to Jaques-Barthélémy. The letter was dated July 5, 1819.

In 1839 Vacheron & Constantin hired Georges-Auguste Leschot. His job was to supervise the manufacturing operations. Leschot was an inventor and his creations turned out to be successful for the company. His inventions had a great impact on the watchmaking industry in general. He was the first person to standardize movements into Calibers.

In 1844 Georges-Auguste Leschot was awarded with a gold medal. The Arts Society of Geneva highly appreciated his pantographic device, a device that was able to mechanically engrave small watch parts and dials. This invention pushed Vacheron & Constantin forward much further than other watchmakers.

Later, after Constantin's death in 1854, and Vacheron's death in 1863, the company was taken over by a series of heirs. At one point, the company was headed by two women.

In 1862 Vacheron Constantin became a member of the Association for Research into non-magnetic materials. Later in 1885, the company created the first nonmagnetic timepiece which included a complete lever assortment made of materials able to withstand magnetic fields. Its construction included a balance wheel, balance spring and lever shaft that were made of palladium, the lever arms - in bronze and the escape wheel was in gold.

In 1877 "Vacheron & Constantin, Fabricants, Geneve" became the official name of the company. In 1880, Vacheron & Constantin started using its symbol, which is kept till nowadays, the Maltese cross. The latter was inspired by a component of the barrel. The part had a cross-shape and it was used for limiting the tension within the mainspring.

In 1887, was reorganized into a stock company. For the remarkable achievements of the company it was awarded with a gold medal at Swiss National Exhibition. The event took place in Geneva in 1887.

The first boutique in Geneva was opened by Vacheron Constantin in 1906. This store can be seen today on Quai de l'Ile. During the Great Depression Vacheron & Constantin found itself in a difficult situation and the only one to bring hope was Charles Constantin. He became the head of the company in 1936 and it was the first time since 1850s that a representative of the Constantin family received the position of Vacheron & Constantin's president.

In 1970 the "&" was dropped from Vacheron & Constantin.

In 1979 Vacheron Constantin made Kallista, one of the most expensive wristwatches. Its initial price was $5 million, but today the watch is valued at about $11 million. Kallista had 118 emerald-cut diamonds. It took about 6,000 hours for the watch masters to make this watch and about 20 months for jewelers to enrich the watch.

When Jacques Ketterer died in 1987, Vacheron Constantin changed hands. However its sales increased and today the company produces about 20,000 timepieces per year. In 1996 the entire share capital of the company was bought by Richemont Group.

In 2003 Vacheron Constantin introduced a new sports line called Overseas, and a collection called Egérie, the first to include watches for women.

In 2004 Vacheron Constantin opened its new headquarters and manufacture in Plan-les-Ouates, Geneva.

The Richemont Group named Juan Carlos Torres as the Chief Executive Officer of the company in October 2005. Vacheron Constantin is considered to be company that was able to create one of the most complicated wristwatches in the world entitled "Tour de I'lle". It was created in 2005 to mark the anniversary of 250 years of Vacheron Constantin. The watch includes 834 parts and 16 horological complications. It was only available through the Vacheron Constantin shop in Geneva, Switzerland and sold for more than $1 million.

In 2007 Vacheron Constantin introduced the Metiers d'Art 'Les Masques' collection of timepieces featuring miniature reproductions of primitive art masks. The company selected twelve masks from a private museum collection and reproduced the masks on a small scale. The miniaturized masks are featured in the dial center of every watch from the 'Les Masques' collection.

See also

- List of watch manufactures

External links

- Official Website [2]
- Official Vacheron Constantin Discussion Forum [3]
- Vacheron Constantin - The Oldest Watchmaking Company? [4] - Disputing the fact that Vacheron Constantin is the oldest watchmaker

Piaget SA

Piaget SA

Industry	Watchmaking and Jewellery
Founded	La Côte-aux-Fées, Switzerland (1874)
Founder(s)	Georges Edouard Piaget
Headquarters	Geneva, Switzerland
Number of locations	Parts: People's Republic of China
Key people	Georges Edouard Piaget (Founder) Yves Piaget (President)
Products	Watches, Jewels
Parent	Richemont
Website	Piaget.com [1]

Piaget SA is a Swiss luxury watchmakers and jewellers, founded in 1874 by Georges Piaget in the village of La Côte-aux-Fées. The company belongs to the Swiss Richemont group, specialists in the luxury goods industry.

The company was founded as a manufacturer of watch movements but began marketing its own line of prestigious watches in the 20th century.

History

Unless otherwise indicated, all information is taken from the brand's website.

The Company's Origins (1874-1942)

In 1874, Georges Edouard Piaget set up his first workshop on the family farm, situated in the small village of La Côte-aux-Fées in the Swiss Jura mountains. Dedicated to crafting pocket watches and high-precision clock movements for prestigious brands, the Piaget name was soon to travel beyond the borders of the Neuchâtel region. In 1911, Timothée Piaget, the son of Georges Piaget, took over the family firm. The Manufacture has been dedicated to the production of wrist watches ever since.

Registered Trademark (1943-1955)

Under the guidance of the founder's grandsons, Gérald and Valentin Piaget, the Piaget brand became a registered trademark in 1943. Since then, the Manufacture at La Côte-aux-Fées has produced its own creations and has undergone considerable international expansion. As a result of this expansion, the family business opened a new factory in 1945, again in La Côte-aux-Fées.

The Ultra-Thin Movement and Jewellery (1956-1963)

In 1957, the *manufacture* at La Côte-aux-Fées brought out the Calibre 9P, the first ultra-thin (2 mm), hand-wound mechanical movement. Then, in 1960, the Piaget watchmakers developed the Calibre12P, the thinnest automatic movement in the world with a thickness of 2.3 mm (made official by an entry in the Guinness Book of Records). The Piaget collection was diversifying. In addition to coin watches, ring watches, brooch watches and cufflink watches, Piaget created their first pieces of jewellery. In 1957, the Emperador men's watch was launched and since it's relaunch in 1999 become one of the brand's emblematic models. The company's expansion led to the opening of a new factory in Geneva, dedicated to jewellery and, in 1959, their first boutique.

Rapid Expansion (1964-1987)

The brand's jewellery would soon achieve world renown thanks to personalities such as Jackie Kennedy, Gina Lollobrigida and Andy Warhol. In 1964, Piaget presented their first watches with dials worked in precious stones: lapis-lazuli, turquoise, onyx and tiger's eye. Piaget then launched the cuff watch, which became a symbol of fine watchmaking. 1976 saw the launch of the Calibre 7P, a quartz movement. The Piaget Polo watch with its avant-garde style, was brought out in 1979 and became one of the brand's iconic models. The Dancer collection, launched in 1986, met with similar success. Under the presidency of Yves Piaget since 1980, Piaget have continued to cultivate the status of "watchmaker-jeweller".

The Merger (1988-2000)

The luxury Vendôme group, now Richemont, purchased the Piaget Manufacture in 1988. In the 1990s, several new collections were launched: Possession, Tanagra, Limelight and Miss Protocole with its interchangeable straps. Regarding watches, Piaget brought out the Altiplano model and in 1999 reinvented one of their classics, the Emperador line. Watchmaking was regrouped in one collection: Black Tie.

A New Movement (2001-2008)

In 2001, a new Piaget Haute Horlogerie *manufacture* was opened in Plan-les-Ouates, just outside Geneva. The movements continued to be produced at La Côte-aux-Fées, the family's historic birthplace. The new building grouped together over 40 professions in the fields of watchmaking and jewellery. The same year, Piaget added a youthful touch to the Polo watch from the 1970s and launched the Magic Reflections collection. The Manufacture developed several lines of mechanical movements and in 2002 brought out the first Piaget Manufacture tourbillon movement, the Calibre 600P, the thinnest tourbillon in the world with 3.5 mm thickness. In 2004, Piaget celebrated the 130th anniversary of their creation.

Craftsmanship

The Manufacture has existed in various forms since 1874 and more than 40 professions are grouped together, from design to delivery of a technically complicated watch or a magnificent jewellery creation.

The Ultra-Thin Movement

The brand is one of the forerunners in the creation of ultra-thin movements with the manual 9P and automatic 12P movements, respectively the thinnest in their category in the world in 1957 and 1960. This has led in more recent years to the modern developments 430P, 450P and 438P, with a thickness of only 2.1 millimetres. These latest innovations are used in the Altiplano line.

The Tourbillon Movement

The Tourbillon movement was developed over a period of more than three years. Resulting from this research is the calibre 600P, the thinnest tourbillon movement in the world (3.5 mm). Its frame is particularly sophisticated: composed of 42 minuscule parts, including three titanium bridges, it weighs just 0.2 grams. The flying tourbillon – mounted on a single axis – is topped by the initial “P”, which adds to the complexity of the poising.

The Tourbillon Skeleton Movement

Piaget's flying tourbillon movement, an emblematic complication, is the thinnest of its kind in the world (3.5 mm). Divided into segments corresponding to each of the 60 seconds, a sunburst guilloche decoration shines out from the tourbillon's frame. The model is in gold and set with precious stones.

The Retrograde Movement

The Calibre 560P is a self-winding mechanical movement, designed, developed and built at the heart of Manufacture Piaget, and boasting a complex retrograde seconds mechanism. The hand traces an arc from 0 to 30 at 12 o'clock, then jumps back to its starting point. The design of the handcrafted finishing details took 24 months: circular Côtes de Genève decoration, stippled main plate, bevelled and hand-drawn bridges as well as blued screws.

The Self-Winding Movement

A new generation of self-winding mechanical movements was launched in 2006. The 800P, with hours, minutes, central seconds hands and large date display, is equipped with two barrels, guaranteeing a power reserve of 72 hours. This 12-ligne calibre, beats at 21,600 vibrations per hour (3 hertz) and its timing is ensured by a screw-regulated balance. The 850P version displays small seconds and a second time zone on two sub-dials. A day/night indicator synchronised with the central time zone completes the display.

The Art of Enamelling

Piaget continue the tradition of miniature painting thanks to a traditional technique. The enameller begins by crushing and cleaning raw enamels to obtain a very fine powder, which is then mixed with essential oils to achieve the colour palette. The enamel is applied with a brush in successive fine layers, each of which is oven-fired at temperatures exceeding 800 °C. Each enamelled piece requires nearly twenty firings in the oven. The enamel and its colours are then set forever.

Setting and Gemmology

Piaget own the largest jewellery workshop in Geneva. Every stone here is cut, adjusted and set by hand. The same attention to detail characterises the selection of diamonds and precious stones. The diamonds, for example, meet the highest standards of colour (D to G) and clarity (IF to VVS.) The diamonds are tested according to stringent in-house guidelines based on their colour, size, clarity and carat. Piaget are members of the "Council for Responsible Jewellery Practices" and the "Kimberley Process Certification Scheme", which guarantees that diamonds do not originate from an area of conflict.

Prizes and Awards

Prizes Awarded

Piaget have received numerous awards over the course of the brand's history:

- In 2000, the jury of Montres Passion awarded the prize of "Watch of the Year" to the Emperador model .
- At the Geneva Watchmaking Grand Prix, the Piaget 1967 watch was awarded the "Design Watch Prize" in 2002 and the Altiplano XL watch won the "Ultra-Flat Watch Prize" in 2003 .
- At the Geneva Watchmaking Grand Prix, Piaget were awarded the Ladies' Jewellery Watch Prize in 2006, for their Limelight Party model .
- In 2006 the Limelight Party watch was also elected "Most beautiful watch of 2006" by the magazine Vogue Joyas Spain .
- The Piaget Polo Chronograph watch was elected "Watch of the Year 2007" in the Chronograph category by the jury of the French magazine La Revue des Montres .
- The Emperador model received the prize of Men's Watch of the Year 2007 (Middle East Watch of the Year Awards 2007), organised by the magazine Alam Assaat Wal Moujawharat .
- The Limelight Party Secret watch was named "Watch of the Year 2007" in the Ladies' Watch category by the Belgian magazine Passion des Montres..

Piaget Best Jeweller Prize

In 2005, Piaget created their Best Jeweller Prize. This prize is awarded to the most deserving student of the Certificat Fédéral de Capacité in watchmaking. Dorian Recordon was the first holder of the qualification to receive this prize.

See also

- List of watch manufactures

External links

- Official Piaget website [2]
- Piaget Pictures [3]
- Kimberley Process Certification Scheme [4]
- Council for Responsible Jewellery Practices [5]
- Fondation de la Haute Horlogerie [6]
- Article in Men's Vogue [7]

Valjoux

Valjoux

ETA/Valjoux 7750.

Valjoux (for *Vallée de Joux*, "Joux Valley") is a Swiss manufacturer of mechanical watch movements. It is known primarily for chronograph ébauche movements that are used in a number of mid- to high-range mechanical watches: The company has been a part of ETA for a number of years and is a member of the Swatch Group. Valjoux is responsible for the design and manufacture of the Valjoux 7750 movement (and variants), an extremely popular movement used in the majority of mechanical chronograph watches on the market today.

Notable watch brands that use base movements manufactured by Valjoux include Omega, Longines, Breitling, Cyma Watches, Oris, Appella, TAG Heuer, IWC, Porsche Design, Gallet, Sinn, Gc, and so on.

External links

- Valjoux Reference Site [1] Excellent source for company history, watch details, etc.
- ofrei.com [2]
- timezone.com [3] The Valjoux 7750 chronograph.
- Alliance Horlogere [4] A page containing information about the Valjoux 7750 along with a video showing the mechanism being assembled

Zeno-Watch Basel

Zeno-Watch Basel

Zeno-Watch is a Swiss watchmaker in business since 1868, but only using the Zeno name since 1922. Specializing in aviation watches, they exist today as one of the few independent Swiss watch manufacturers still in operation, and make watches in their factory in Basel, Switzerland. Some lower-end watches, however, are manufactured in Japan.

The Zeno *Nostalgia*, an aviation watch with chronograph function, date and day of the week, with a 1920-style finish

External links

- Official site [1] (www.zeno-watch.ch)

Zenith (watchmaker)

Zenith (watchmaker)

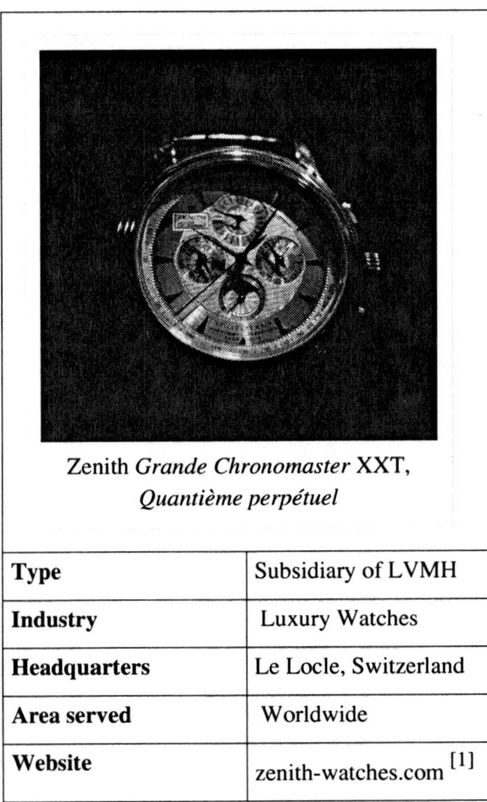

Zenith *Grande Chronomaster* XXT, *Quantième perpétuel*

Type	Subsidiary of LVMH
Industry	Luxury Watches
Headquarters	Le Locle, Switzerland
Area served	Worldwide
Website	zenith-watches.com [1]

Zenith SA is a Swiss watch *manufacture* started in 1865 by Georges Favre-Jacot at the age of 22, in Le Locle in the canton of Neuchâtel.

Zenith has a long reputation for the quality and precision of their watches, with 1,565 1st-place precision awards to date. Zenith, is one of the few Swiss watch brands that make their own mechanical movements - the *Elite* (standard movement) and the *El Primero* (chronograph). The El Primero movement has a frequency of 36,000 alternations per hour. This high rate allows a resolution of 1/10th of a second and a potential for greater positional accuracy over the more typical chronometer frequency of 28,000 alt per hour.

History

Zenith was purchased by luxury giant LVMH in November 1999, becoming one of several brands in LVMH's watch and jewelry division.

Products

Presently, Zenith markets five watch lines, including the Chronomaster, Class, Port-Royal, Vintage, Defy, Star and the all new Omnipotence.

Photo gallery

See also

- List of watch manufactures

External links

- Zenith official website [1]

Baume et Mercier

Baume et Mercier

History

After World War II

After World War II Baume et Mercier concentrated on conventional men's watches, sports chronographs and ladies' jewellery watches. In 1965 the Piaget family bought control over Baume et Mercier. One of the world's thinnest calendar watches with a mini rotor was produced under Piaget's aegis. In the same year the new owners switched to electronic tuning fork movements, and from 1970 increased investments in quartz movements. At the end of the 1983, Baume et Mercier temporarily ceased production of mechanical watches. In 1988, Christian and Yves Piaget sold 60% of their stake to Piaget holding S.A., also selling Baume et Mercier S.A. to Cartier Monde S.A. in Paris. In 1993 the Cartier group became sole owners of both Piaget and Baume et Mercier.

Recent times

- Member of the American Watch Guild

Old models

- Classiqe
- Riviera Baumematik
- Shogun
- Formula
- Marquis
- Malibu
- Avant Garde
- Medicus

- Transpacific

Model Malibu By Baume et Mercier
produced during 1990's

Riviera

One of the company's most successful watches was the Riviera, launched in 1973. This was a sports watch with distinctive gold and steel features and an unusual 12 sided bezel. To test its durability and precision, this watch was mounted on the wheel of a BMW M1 before the start of the Le Mans 24-hours race. It withstood high speeds as well as the pressure of fast acceleration. It was not affected by the centrifugal force of spinning wheels, nor by heavy rainfall or intense heat from the overworked disk brakes. At the end of the race the watch ran with as much precision as it had at the beginning.

New models

- Hampton Classic
- Hampton Classic
- Hampton Classic Diamond
- Hampton Milleis Chronograph
- Hampton Milleis Gold
- Hampton Milleis
- Hampton City Chronograph
- Hampton City
- Hampton Spirit

- Capeland S Chronograph
- Capeland S Ladies
- Capeland S Ladies Diamond
- Classima Executives XL Dual Time
- Classima Executives XL Small Seconds
- Classima Executives White Dial
- Classima Executives Black Dial
- Classima Subsidiary Seconds
- Classima Sweep Seconds
- Linea
- Riviera
- Vice Versa
- Diamant
- Selector
- Haute Joaillerie collection
- Iléa

Gallery

A rare obsoleted watch branded "LeRoy" manufactured by Baume-et-Mercier During 1980's

External links

- Baume & Mercier Official Website [1]
- History of Baume & Mercier [2]

Movado

Movado

Type	Public (NYSE: MOV [1])
Founded	La Chaux-de-Fonds, Switzerland (1881)
Founder(s)	Achille Ditesheim
Headquarters	Paramus, New Jersey, United States
Key people	Efraim Grinberg, Chairman and CEO
Products	Watches
Revenue	▼US$460,857,000 (2009)
Operating income	▼US$3,288,000 (2009)
Net income	▼US$2,552,000 (2009)
Total assets	▼US$440,000,000 (2009)
Website	http://www.movado.com/

Movado is a Swiss luxury watch company whose name is Esperanto for "always in motion". Movado was founded in 1881 in La Chaux-de-Fonds, Switzerland by Achilles Ditesheim. The company was purchased by arts enthusiast Gedalio Grinberg of New York in 1983; his son, Efraim Grinberg, is the current Chairman and Chief Executive Officer of Movado Group, Inc. The North American President of Movado and ESQ by Movado is Alan Chinich.

The company is known for its iconic *Museum Watch* which is defined by a single gold dot symbolizing the sun at high noon, the hands suggesting the movement of the earth. The original Museum Watch was the first wrist watch to be displayed at the Museum of Modern Art and was designed by the American designer Nathan George Horwitt in 1947. Edward Steichen, the rewnowned photographer and director of the photography department at New York's Museum of Modern Art, proclaimed Horwitt's design "the only truly original and beautiful one for such an object".

Movado commissioned the design and installation of "Time Sculpture". This unique clock sculpture was designed by world renowned architect Philip Johnson. It is located outside Lincoln Center in New York City. In 2006, Movado celebrated its 125th year of watchmaking.

Movado Group, Inc. designs, manufactures, and distributes Movado, Ebel, Concord, ESQ by Movado, Coach, Hugo Boss, Lacoste, Juicy Couture and Tommy Hilfiger watches worlwide.

External links

- G Grinberg's Obituary in the New York Times [2]
- ESQ by Movado [3]

Ulysse Nardin

Ulysse Nardin

Type	Private company
Industry	Watch manufacturing
Founded	1846 by Ulysse Nardin
Headquarters	, Le Locle, Switzerland
Website	Ulysse Nardin [1]

Ulysse Nardin is a watch manufacturer founded in 1846 in Le Locle, Switzerland. Historically Ulysse Nardin was best known for being a manufacturer of marine chronometers, but today Ulysse Nardin produces complicated mechanical watches.

History

Founder, watchmaker Ulysse Nardin, was an accomplished watchmaker who studied horology under his father, Leonard-Frederic Nardin, Frederic William Dubois, and Louis Jean Richard-dit-Bressel, in Switzerland.

The Modern Era

In 1983, Ulysse Nardin was acquired by businessman Rolf Schnyder who, in conjunction with watchmaker Ludwig Oechslin, relaunched the brand with other investors. Schnyder, Oechslin and the staff of Ulysse Nardin, design and create complication timepieces using modern materials and manufacturing techniques. The base movement used on all version of complication watches is the ETA. The new ETA 2892 movement, used by Ulysse Nardin in the New collection, is enormously popular because it is deemed accurate and reliable enough to be used as a base movement for many high-end manufacturers' complications. Most changes and updates were done in order to improve the efficiency of the automatic winding. The beat rate has been increased to 28,800 BPH, while the diameter of the movement was reduced from 28mm to 25.6mm to allow it to be used in a wider range of cases. (Hence, the change in model number from 2890 to 2892.) The thickness, however, remains unchanged at 3.6 mm. This has the effect of reducing both the diameter and mass of the oscillating weight that was fixed in the 2892/A2 model. The 9mm diameter balance compromises between weight and size. The first example of Ulysse Nardin's new approach was the *Astrolabium Galileo Galilei* (1985, named after the device, Astrolabium, and the astronomer, Galileo). The Astrolabium displays local and solar time, the orbits and eclipses of the sun and the moon, and the positions of several major stars. It was named by the Guinness Book of Records in 1989 as the world's most functional watch (with 21 distinct functions). Oechslin followed the *Astrolabium* with two other astronomical watches, the *Planetarium Copernicus* (1988, named after the stargazing theaters called planetariums and the astronomer Copernicus) and the *Tellurium Johannes Kepler* (1992, named after the element tellurium, and astronomer, Johannes Kepler,). The three pieces constitute what the brand calls the *Trilogy of Time*.

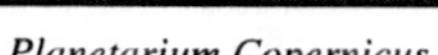

Planetarium Copernicus

Astrolabium Galileo Galilei

Tellurium Johannes Kepler

Other notable complication watches are the *GMT± Perpetual* (1999), that combines a perpetual calendar with the GMT± complication (one-press buttons that adjust the hour hand back and forth for international travellers), and the *Freak Blue Phantom* (2001) a tourbillon watch with no crown and one mechanical hands that cranks along teeth embeded in the inner circumference of the watch face.

External links

- Ulysse Nardin website [1]

Ulysse Nardin Marine Chronometer 1846.

Chopard

Chopard

Type	Privately held company
Industry	Watch manufacturing
Founded	1867 by Louis-Louis Chopard
Headquarters	Geneva, Switzerland
Products	Wristwatches, accessories
Website	Chopard.com [1]

Chopard is a Swiss based luxury watch, jewelry, and accessories company founded in 1860 by Louis-Ulysse Chopard at the age of 24. Chopard initially concentrated on developing precise pocket watches and chronometers based upon innovative ideas. Chopard is regarded as a *manufacture*, in other words that they make many of their watches and movements in-house rather than using the base movements (ebauches) of other manufacturers. Chopard, which also has production facilities in Fleurier, is one of four participating brands in the Fleurier Quality Foundation (together with Bovet, Parmigiani and Vaucher), which certifies a very high level of quality to manufactured watches (www.fleurier-quality.com). The "Qualité Fleurier" standard is meant to compete with the Geneva standards such as the exclusive Geneva Seal manufacturing standard.

History

In 1963 the Chopard Company was taken over by the young goldsmith and watchmaker Karl Scheufele, after Paul-Andre Chopard, the last master watchmaker who maintained the horological roots of the family, was forced to give up the business since his sons, following other careers, refused to manage the business. Paul-Andre agreed to sell the business to Karl Scheufele, who as the new head of the company, gained significant experience with watchmaking and jewelry making. He contributed to modernization of the company and added the jewelry segment into the Chopard watch production.

In 1975 the Chopard factory moved from the center of Geneva to Meyrin-Geneva. It marked a new stage for the company as it started producing ladies' and jewelry timepieces. In 1976 Chopard introduced the Happy Diamonds collection. Watches from the collection featured mobile diamonds that floated freely between two transparent sapphire crystals.

In 1980 the Chopard Company debuted with sports watches on leather straps. The range of Happy Diamonds watches was enlarged by jewelry pieces. The first Chopard boutiques were opened in Hong Kong, Geneva and Vienna in the 1980-s.

In 1988 Chopard established the cooperation with the Mille Miglia, an annual Italian rally where vintage and classic cars take part. To mark the partnership, Chopard has maintained the tradition of developing a new special edition Mille Miglia timepiece every year.

The Chopard Happy Sport collection appeared in 1993.

In 1996, the Chopard Company opened its independent movement factory in Fleurier.

Also in 1996, after years of planning and development, the first Chopard in-house movement of the late 20th century was produced, the calibre 1.96, encased in the "1860" hunter-back case, named for the historical origins of the manufacture. This was to be the flagship watch of Chopard, their re-entree as it were to manufacture status, and Chopard spared no effort with it. Only 300 of the 1860 hunter-back units are known to have been produced. However, the calibre 1.96 was incorporated into later iterations of the 1860 watch without the hunter-back. Many of these 1860 watches, called "16/1860/2" and "16/1860/3" and all without hunter-backs, were produced. The calibre 1.96 achieved a level of design and finish that set it apart and qualified it as haute horlogerie in many ways. It was stamped with the Geneva Seal which is a designation reserved for the highest level of construction and finish, incorporated a 22k micro-rotor into a very thin (3.3 mm) movement and with a unique bi-directional winding mechanism, had twin mainspring barrels allowing for a 65 hour power reserve, a breguet overcoil hairspring and a swan-neck micro regulator. It had 32 jewels and ran at 28,800 beats per hour. It was found to be a highly accurate movement. The calibre 1.96 was in many ways a ground-breaking movement for Chopard. Walt Odets wrote a comprehensive technical review of the 1.96 movement (see link below). It has been referred to as perhaps the finest Swiss automatic movement now produced.

In 1998 the Company partnered with the annual Cannes International Film Festival. In 2000 the beginning of the new millennium was marked by the introduction of the Chopard L.U.C Quattro watch, powered by a technically advanced caliber with four barrels - an innovation that provided 9-day power reserve.

In 2001 the horology world was joined by the Chopard L.U.C Tonneau watch powered by the first-ever tonneau-shaped self-winding movement with off-centered micro-rotor. In 2002 Chopard new Golden Diamonds concept enlarged the jewelry range.

In 2003 the Chopard Tourbillon watch enlarged the Manufacture's L.U.C. range and the Happy Spirit collection was born. In 2004 the Company unveiled the L.U.C. Regulateur watch and the Butterfly jewelry pieces collection. In 2005 ,Chopard presented the Copacabana and Golden Diamonds collections and introduced the L.U.C. Lunar 1. The brand became a part of the sailing world, having initiated the Grand Prix Chopard Decision 35 sailing regatta.

In 2006 the company celebrated the 30th anniversary of Happy Diamonds watch collection and the 10th anniversary of the movement factory in Fleurier.

Mr. Scheufele is still the president of the Chopard Company. He has kept the Company as a family business. In the 1990s his children joined the business. Caroline Scheufele is the head of the jewelry division, while Karl-Friedrich manages the watchmaking department.

Chopard holds three production sites located in Geneva, Fleurier in Switzerland and Pforzheim in Germany. The Company has organized its products distribution through 13 subsidiaries placed all over the world. In addition, the brand has opened over 90 brand boutiques.

By 2007, the United States has Chopard boutiques in New York City, Beverly Hills and Costa Mesa, California, Bal Harbour and Palm Beach, Florida,and Old San Juan, Puerto Rico. A ninth boutique will open in Boston in 2008 and in San Francisco in 2008 as well. There are hundreds of Chopard Authorized retailers in the United States, and thousands worldwide in every major world city like in Kuala Lumpur.

Watch collections

The Chopard Company has developed a variety of watch collections, including quartz and mechanical timepieces, gem-set and technically complicated models, classic and sporty ones. The list of the leading Chopard collections is the following: Mille Miglia, L.U.C., Happy Diamonds, Happy Sport, Happy Spirit, Classiques, Your Houre, La Strada and Haute Horlogerie.

Chopard Mille Miglia watch collection comprises mechanical timepieces of sporty style. These timepieces appeared as a result of the brand's partnership with Italian car rally, the Mille Miglia. The Chopard Happy Sport ladies' collection features timepieces that unite sporty style with precious stones and bright colors. The L.U.C collection features massive sporty-styled chronometers and elegant classy men's watches.

Charity

Chopard has contributed to the development of medical research, taken part in different charitable events and helped a number of foundations, including the Elton John AIDS Foundation. Chopard has continuously cooperated in fight against AIDS with Sir Elton John who established the foundation in 1993 and still holds the post of its Chairman. The brand launches limited-edition Elton John watches to benefit the foundation. Chopard co-sponsors the charity events annually held by the foundation - Elton John AIDS Foundation Oscar Party, White Tie & Tiara Ball and An Enduring Vision.

Caroline Scheufele, presently the co-president of Chopard worldwide, is responsible for supporting other charity organizations such as the International José Carreras Foundation involved in the fight against leukemia and the Sabrina foundation for sick children. The Sheufele family is also involved with The Prince Charles of Wales foundation donating timeless Chopard pieces as a symbol of their dedication to the Prince's cause .

Partnership

- The Chopard Company and New York William Goldberg Diamond Corporation have established a close partnership. William Goldberg is found among the major suppliers of precious stones worldwide.

William Goldberg Diamond Corporation is responsible for recreating a classic diamond cut named the Ashoka. The cut is based on the distinguished original Ashoka diamond that represented a 41.37 carats (8.27 g) D flawless diamond. The gem inherited its name after Ashoka Maurya, the Hindu warrior-emperor. It was mined in southern India. The diamond is special for its unique cut and superior aesthetic characteristics received legendary status over the years. The William Goldberg Ashoka trademarked was patented by William Goldberg Corp. in 2000. In 2006 Chopard initiated the production of a new line of luxury watches set with Ashoka diamonds to be supplied by William Goldberg Diamond Corp. The new Chopard Ashoka Watch Collection will comprise six timepieces set with the rare diamonds,crimeajewel.

- Member of the American Watch Guild

Chopard at Cannes Festival

The partnership between the Chopard Company and the Cannes Film Festival started in 1997. It was initiated by the meeting between Caroline Gruosi-Scheufele, Chopard Co-President, and Pierre Viot, President of the festival. By Viot's request, Mrs. Gruosi-Scheufele with the team of Chopard master craftsmen redesigned the Golden palm award. The Palme d'Or redesigned by Chopard was unveiled on May 24, 1998.

The partnership between Chopard and the Cannes Film Festival continued with Chopard's introduction of a new award to promote creativity in films. Since 2001, the Chopard Trophy has been awarded to two young actors as Male and Female Revelation of the Year.

To mark the 60th Anniversary of the festival, for the Cannes Film Festival 2007 opening ceremony the Chopard Company developed the Red Carpet Collection in cooperation with Valentino. Caroline Scheufele created 60 high jewellery pieces inspired by the celebrities at Cannes, while Valentino designed ten gowns to complement ten of the company's jewels.

See also

- List of watch manufactures

References

Walt Odets, From the House of Happy Diamonds: The Chopard L.U.C. Caliber 1.96 http://www.timezone.com/library/horologium/horologium631672821689171141

External links

- Official site [1]

Audemars Piguet

Audemars Piguet

Industry	Watch manufacturing
Products	Wristwatches, accessories
Website	www.audemarspiguet.com/ [1]

Audemars Piguet is a *manufacture* of expensive Swiss watches which compete with Patek Philippe, Jaeger-LeCoultre, and Vacheron Constantin.

Foundation

Thus Audemars started producing component parts for movements and Piguet got the job of a *repasseur,* whose job it was to make the final regulation of the timepiece. They founded a firm later known as **Audemars, Piguet et Cie**.

Since 1882, members of the Audemars and Piguet families have always been on the board of directors and have thus directly or indirectly run the company.

Business

The business started with Audemars managing the production and technical part and Piguet focusing on sales, and success was not immediate. The Audemars Piguet trademark was registered in 1882, however it would be seven years later that the company was officially founded. At this point Audemars Piguet et Cie became one of the largest employers for watch-making in the whole of Vaud, southwestern Switzerland.

The company opened its first branch in Geneva in 1889, and began creating its own components and assembling within its factory with direct supervision and strict quality control .

Between 1894 and 1899 the company produced about 1,200 timepieces, including some very complex watches. When Audemars and Piguet died, in 1918 and 1919 respectively, the company steadily grew and became more famous. As the success of the company's business was rising its customers became Tiffany & Co, Cartier and Bulgari, who rebranded and sold Audemars Piguet watches under their own house names. Today these watches are only identifiable as Audemars Piguet products by their serial numbers.

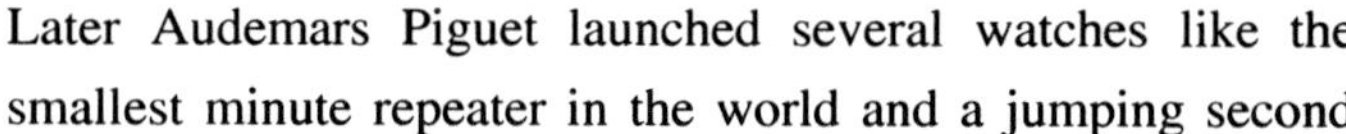

Later Audemars Piguet launched several watches like the smallest minute repeater in the world and a jumping second hand (i.e. the second hand jumps from second to second in quanta rather than progressively) pocket watch. In 1925 Audemars Piguet introduced the world's thinnest pocket watch, at 1.32 millimeters. Only three years later the company created the first skeleton watch.

At the end of 1920s and the beginning of 1930s the success of Audemars Piguet started dimming. The crash of the stock market as well as the Depression slowed the development of many Swiss companies.

During World War II the manufacturer was able to come back on the market by producing one of its well-known models – an ultra-thin chronograph, the heart of which was Calibre 2003. The sales of Audemars Piguet started growing in the forties and fifties. Together with Jaeger-LeCoultre it designed the thinnest automatic movement. The latter included a 21 carat gold rotor placed in the center. Their "Royal Oak", was produced in 1972 and is considered to have created the market for the stainless steel luxury watch. It was designed by Gerald Genta.

The Audemars Piguet watch group is composed of 1,100 employees, fourteen distribution subsidiaries and sixteen boutiques around the world. It comprises three production sites: Le Brassus (SA de la Manufacture d'Horlogerie Audemars Piguet & Cie), LeLocle (Audemars Piguet: Renaud et Papi SA) and Meyrin (Center SA).

The manufacture Audemars Piguet produces 26,000 timepieces per year.

Sponsorships

Since 1999, Audemars Piguet has been the sponsor of the Queen Elizabeth II Cup, a Group One Thoroughbred horse race in Hong Kong, New Territories, China.

Audemars Piguet are also a sponsor of the Alinghi Sailing Team which won the America's Cup in 2003 & 2007

In 2007, Audemars Piguet offered its support to the Clinton Foundation. The Foundation works around the world on global issues, including education, health, poverty issues, and fight against HIV/AIDS. The company created the Jules Audemars Clinton Foundation Equation of Time watch in a limited edition of 126 pieces. The watch incorporated complex astronomical features. It shows sunrise and sunset times, perpetual calendar and astronomical moon.

Ambassadors

Like many other brands of luxury watches, Audemars Piguet has a number of ambassadors, such as Indonesian-French singer Anggun, Indian Cricketer Sachin Tendulkar and Malaysian actress Michelle Yeoh, as well personalities and teams in different sport categories such as cricket, softball, golf, skiing, motor sports and sailing.

In media

In the HBO series, *Entourage*, Ari Gold receives an Audemars Piguet watch as a promotional gift from John Ellis, the fictional chairman of the parent company that owns Universal Pictures. Ellis describes it as "perhaps, the finest timepiece in the world".

In the movie Quick Change, starring Bill Murray, one of the hostages offers up a Audemars Piguet watch in hopes of being the next person to be released. Bill Murray trades him his Timex with a Twist-o-Flex band by Speidel, plus $300.

The Audemars Piguet Royal Oak Offshore T3 was featured in the movie Terminator 3: Rise of the Machines.

The 2010 Swedish House Mafia single "Miami 2 Ibiza", featuring Tinie Tempah, opens with the lyric "She says she likes my watch, but she wants Steve's AP", referencing the fact that Angello wears an Audemar Piguet Royal Oak Offshore wristwatch.

See also

- List of watch manufactures

External links

- Official site [1]
- Latest News on Audemars Piguet [2]
- History of Audemars Piguet [3]
- Emblematic models of Audemars Piguet [4]
- Audemars Piguet on Youtube [5]
- Article on Audemars Piguet, Le Brassus [6]

Titoni

Titoni

TITONI LTD. is a Swiss watch company which was founded in 1919 by Fritz Schluep in the city of Grenchen. Nowadays the company is still in family property and employs around 50 workers. Since its foundation, the watches are sold mainly in the Asian and Middle East market.

History

In the year 1851, the watch-making industry was introduced to the small city of Grenchen Switzerland. Many famous watch companies were founded here and have helped make Grenchen an important part of today's Swiss watch business.

Today, the Titoni Company is in its third generation of family ownership. New to the US market, Titoni has concentrated on the far east and near east markets for over 50 years.

While many watch brands have focused over the last twenty-five years on quartz watches, Titoni has continued in the niche it has always occupied: watches equipped with self-winding mechanical movements. All Titoni watch components have to fulfill rigorous quality standards. The components for automatic movements, such as jeweled lever escapements, main springs, jewel shock absorbers, etc., are individually selected. This is claimed to assure better quality in contrast to other watch companies who buy complete movements. The assembly and integration of movements, as well as finishing and final control of the complete watches are handled at the Titoni factory in Switzerland.

Standard Titoni features include sapphire crystals, water resistance from 30 meters up to 200 meter, solid bracelets, buckles with two push-pieces and the stones on the dials are individually set, not glued. The modern Titoni factory makes use of manufacturing technology including extensive automation.

Franck Muller

Franck Muller

Industry	Watch manufacturing
Headquarters	Geneva, Switzerland
Key people	Franck Muller
Website	www.franckmullerusa.com [1]

Franck Muller (born July 1958) is a noted Swiss watchmaker known for creating complicated timepieces. His brand of watches carries the slogan, "Master of Complications".

Franck Muller watches are worn by various celebrities, among them: Demi Moore, Robin Williams, Elton John, 50 Cent, and José Mourinho.

Franck Muller timepieces are famous for their fusion of "modern" style (mostly inspired by American watches from the thirties, like Elgin tonneau) and traditional Swiss watch manufacturing. The president of the company that holds its name is a watchmaker himself. He claims to design the mechanism of every watch by himself.

Biography

Franck Muller was born in 1958. He spent his childhood in La Chaux-de-Fonds with his Italian mother and Swiss-born father. When 15, he enrolled in a watchmaking school.

In the early 1980s, he graduated from the Swiss school of watchmaking (French: *Ecole d'Horlogerie de Genève*). Afterwards he began repairing top-quality pocket watches. Close to an independent watchmaker by the name of Svend Andersen, Franck Muller became responsible for handling watches from the collection of Patek Philippe.

Most of the clientele were private individuals and museums. While he was working with complicated timepieces, he became passionate about their mechanisms and began to think of building his own workshop.

Business

Very soon, in 1984, Franck Muller designed his own tourbillon wristwatch. In the 1980s, few watchmakers were capable of creating such complicated timepieces, among them Patek Philippe and Vacheron Constantin. The private clients of Franck Muller continued to come for new timepieces and thus his business started growing.

The House of Franck Muller opened in 1991 and his ultra complicated timepieces instantly became famous in Europe and the United States. Today his factory, which is also the headquarters of Franck Muller, produces a limited number of watches for private clientele. Today, Franck Muller's collections include a variety of designs and price ranges.

He thought of building a factory in the heart of Genthod, a village situated outside of Geneva. Surrounded by a vineyard-covered hill and Lake Geneva, he is continuously inspired to create new original, complicated and exclusive watches.

He knows that the first thing that catches the eye of the client is the design of a watch. This is why he created a well-known Curvex Tonneau case, easily recognizable on any wrist. Today, collections of watches from Franck Muller include: Chronograph, Color Dreams, Tourbillon and Conquistador Cortez King.

World Premieres

Franck Muller is also known for its "World Premiers". Each year, the manufacturer launches at least one new line of timepieces featuring something special and exclusive, that has never seen before in the watchmaking industry. The first such world premiere was launched in 1993. It had split seconds chronograph minute repeater as well as a perpetual calendar. In addition, it included an indicator showing the internal temperature.

Many of the world premieres from Franck Muller are patented. All his watches are mechanical, having either a manual or self-winding movements. Some of their watches use movements based on standard ETA calibers.

Notable timepieces include Revolution2, Revolution3, Crazy Hours and Colour Dreams. Further examples of Franck Muller's watches include the Endurance, which is a simple chronograph, the Master Banker, which is a tonneau-shaped watch capable of multiple time zone indication, and the Curvex Minute Repeater Tourbillon, whose production is limited to 25 pieces.

Notable timepieces

- Aeternitas
- Revolution2
- Revolution3
- Crazy Hours
- Color Dreams
- Casablanca
- Conquistador

External links

- Official US website [1]
- Official UK website [2]
- Official Japanese website [3]
- Interview with Franck Muller [4]
- Franck Muller [5] - designer profile at Fashion Model Directory

Rotary Watches

Rotary Watches

Type	Privately held company
Industry	Watch movement & case manufacturing
Founded	1895 by Moise Dreyfuss
Headquarters	Regent Street, London, United Kingdom
Key people	Robert Dreyfuss (Chairman)
Products	Wristwatches, accessories
Website	Rotary Official Website [1]

Rotary Watches Ltd. was established at La Chaux-de-Fonds, Switzerland by Moise Dreyfuss in 1895. By the 1920s family members Georges and Sylvain Dreyfuss began importing Rotary watches to Britain, which was to become the company's most successful market. Rotary is still an independent family company, and at present Robert Dreyfuss – the great grandchild of Moise Dreyfuss – is its chairman.

In 1940 Rotary became the official watch supplier for the British Army. Coinciding as this did with the Second World War and the drafting of huge numbers into the army, the move put a Rotary watch in almost every household in Britain, leaving a lasting impression of the brand in the UK. More recently, Rotary Watches was elected as one of the UK's "superbrands" in 2006 and has retained its place in successive years. The "winged wheel" Rotary logo was first introduced in 1925 and has since undergone only minor changes in appearance. In addition to its traditional brand, the company also produces watches under the more exclusive "Dreyfuss & Co" name.

Rotary is a member of the Federation of the Swiss Watch Industry FH. Although naturally proud of their Swiss heritage, Rotary Watches' head office is now in the UK, and they are predominately a British company. As is the case with many watchmakers, Rotary offer a range of timepieces manufactured in Switzerland together with a range of less expensive pieces made elsewhere, usually with movements from Japan or China.

Rotary watches typically use either a quartz or automatic movement, and often feature what Rotary refer to as the "Dolphin Standard" (equivalent to at least ISO 2281), meaning they are water resistant and may be suitable for all-day swimming and diving. Unique to Rotary is the "Revelation" design of reversible watch, which features two distinct movements and faces, allowing the wearer to change style at will or easily switch between two different time zones.

External links

- Rotary Watches [2]
- Federation of the Swiss Watch Industry FH [3]

Rado (watch)

Rado (watch)

History

Rado Silver Star, circa 1980

Formed in 1917 as Schlup & Co., Rado initially produced watch movements only. In 1957 the company launched its first collection of watches under the Rado brand. In 1962 the Rado Diastar, the world's first scratch-proof watch, was launched. It has been in production ever since, now sold as DiaStar The Original.

In 1983 Rado became part of the SMH group which was renamed in 1998 as the Swatch Group. Rado's sister brands within the Group include Omega, Breguet, Hamilton, Longines and Tissot.

Design

RADO differs from the traditional Swiss watch makers in that it leans towards innovative uses of high tech materials in distinct design. RADO has focused on pioneering the use of a number of materials that are unique within the watch making industry, such as e.g. hardmetal(tungsten- and titanium-carbide), ceramics, lanthanum and sapphire crystal.

In 2004 the RADO vision was realized with the introduction of the V10K. Coating the watch with high tech diamonds made the V10K the hardest watch on Earth, realized by the Guinness Book of World Records.

The newer RADO watches are also distinct from the traditional Swiss watch industry in that their aesthetic is unique. Market reaction tends to be mixed to such a strong aesthetic, with many who appreciate the unique and distinct RADO look and those who do not.

During their time, RADO has received more than 20 elite international design awards, from the RED DOT Award to the iF Design Award, for both their product and most recently, their collaboration with Jasper Morrison for an innovative watch box that mimics the shape of the human wrist.

Pricing

RADO watches vary in pricing according to model, age and materials but the core collection of RADO pieces will range from about US$700 to about US$28,000. Models that include pave dials of diamonds and baguette diamonds can cost approximately US $30,000 to $250,000.

External links

- Rado- International Site [1]
- The Swatch Group [3]
- Equation of Time Rado Forum [2]
- Rado-related articles and vintage collection [3]
- Private fan site and vintage collection [4]
- Rado Watch Archive [5] Gallery of Rado Watches with detailed descriptions, brief histories & actual photos

Invicta Watch Group

Invicta Watch Group

Type	Watch Maker
Industry	Watch Design and Marketing
Founded	1837
Headquarters	Hollywood, FL
Key people	Abraham Lalo, Owner Eyal Lalo, CEO Gany Lalo-Cohen, VP Roxsana Guzman, Asst. Mgr.
Products	Wristwatches, accessories
Website	www.invictawatch.com [1]

Invicta Watch Group is a Florida-based fashion watch company, trading on the name, but a distinct entity from the company founded in 1837 by Raphael Picard in La Chaux-de-fonds, Switzerland. The Picard family owned and operated the company until 1991, when the company was purchased by a United States-based investment company. The corporate headquarters were relocated to Hollywood, Florida, where the company also operates its service call center. Panama-born Eyal Lalo, who formerly had some association with Invicta marketing in South America, is the CEO of the company and frequently appears on televised ShopNBC programs.

History

Invicta meaning "invincible" in Vulgar Latin, was designed to bring common people Swiss watches at affordable prices. The company began its history in La Chaux-de-fonds, Switzerland. Swiss watches have been highly prized in many parts of the world, and Invicta watches capitalized in that popularity. Electronic watches like Casio and Timex known as the "quartz invasion" of the 1970s pushed Invicta watches out of popularity. Invicta watches all but disappeared.

In 1991, new management took over product design and continued to market watches under the Invicta banner. Apart from the Invicta brand, the Invicta Watch Group is also responsible for the S. Coifman, Potger-Pietri, Activa, Brizo, Cacciato & Joss, Pastorelli, and Technica lines.

Watches

Invicta watches are made and assembled on several continents: Parts labeled today as "Swiss", are actually made in China, and is one major reason for concerns about the company. Most, if not all of the watches made by Invicta today are of Swiss parts and assembled in whatever location brings back the best return on their investment dollar. Some ostensibly "Swiss Made" watches are still available, but marketing has a tendency to confuse prospective buyers of where the watches are actually made, by stating categorically that some are "hand assembled" in Swiss factories (of which Invicta has no known holdings) and alternatively indicating that other watches are assembled by lessor skilled laborers in far eastern countries. By law, Far East made watches are required to be labeled on the dial with the country of origin of their movement. Invicta utilizes some Chinese-produced versions of Swiss calibers (which may contain Swiss-derived parts), such as ETA, Sellita [2], RONDA [3], ISA [4] and also Citizen/Miyota (Japanese) movements in their product lines. Invicta has indicated they are developing their own proprietary movements upon the purchase of **Technica Swiss Ebauche**, but analysis of these movements shows that they are rebranded, Chinese-produced [5] mechanisms.

Invicta uses as a principle outlet for their watches, hour long blocks of programing, sometimes played back to back on ShopNBC television, and also on their web site at www.shopnbc.com.

The company currently holds an unfavorable rating of over 30% or a grade of F from the Better Business Bureau. and averages hundreds of complaints each week at the Internet forum and 113 formal complaints [6] at the BBB over the past 36 months.

The Invicta Watch Group also markets products besides watches including hats and bags.

External links

- Invicta Watch Group [1]

Alpina Watches

Alpina Watches

Type	Aktiengesellschaft
Industry	Watch manufacturing
Founded	1883 by Gottlieb Hauser
Headquarters	Geneve, Switzerland
Products	Wristwatches
Website	alpina-watches.com [1]

Alpina Watches International SA is a manufacturer of wrist watches based in Plan-les-Ouates, Geneva, Switzerland. The company was founded in 1883 by Gottlieb Hauser, watchmaker in Winterthur, who founded the Swiss Watchmakers Corporation ("Union Horlogère Suisse"). A number of watchmakers joined to purchase watch components and organized their manufacturing. All representatives of Union Horlogère depended on the Association, which aimed to sell high quality watches under the Alpina brand. Quickly, the new concept gained acceptance. Together with qualified manufactures, the Association started to develop its own calibres and to enlarge its distribution network.

Everything ran well until the seventies, when the quartz crises violently crushed the Swiss watch-industry. Alpina was powerless to counter the overwhelming emergence of electronic watches. Other major brands got together to form groups (predecessor of the Swatch Group), but Alpina tried to fight it alone without really succeeding. In 1972, Alpina Watch International SA was incorporated with new German investors, which purchased all shares in Alpina Union Horlogère SA. In 2002, Alpina Watch International SA was acquired by Frederique Constant SA and Alpina watches were relaunched worldwide.

Named "Régulateur 1883" in reference to the year Alpina was founded, Alpina introduced a new model in 2005 as a fitting tribute to the long and rich tradition of the Geneva-based brand. The "regulator" dial is distinguished by the off-centred hour display at 10 o'clock, an exclusive Alpina feature.

In 2008, Alpina Genève celebrated its 125th anniversary with the inauguration of the first movement to be made entirely in its own workshops.

External links

- Alpina website [2]
- Swiss Watch History [3]
- Alpina retailer [4]

Sources

- The Federation of the Swiss Watch Industry(FH) Information Center [5]
- Timezone Article [6]
- International Watch Club [7]

Jaeger-LeCoultre

Jaeger-LeCoultre

Jaeger-LeCoultre (**JLC**) is a luxury watch and clock manufacturer based in Le Sentier, Vaud, Switzerland. Jaeger-LeCoultre has long tradition of supplying movements and parts to other prestige watches companies in Switzerland.

régulateur à tourbillon

History

Founding

In 1833, Antoine LeCoultre (1803–1881) founded a small workshop in Le Sentier, Switzerland, for the manufacture of high-quality timepieces. In 1844, he measured the micrometre (μm) for the first time and created the world's most precise measuring instrument, the millionometer, capable of measuring to thousandths of a millimetre. In 1847, LeCoultre developed a system that eliminated the need for keys to rewind and set watches, using a push-piece that activated a lever to change from one function to another. In 1851, he was awarded a gold medal for his work on timepiece precision and mechanization at the first Universal Exhibition in London.

Jaeger-LeCoultre Master Control: *réserve de marche*, date on hand.

LeCoultre Manufacture

Antoine's son, Elie LeCoultre, desired to control all stages of timepiece production, so in 1866 he transformed his workshop into a *manufacture*, allowing his employees to pool their expertise under one roof. In 1870, LeCoultre began using mechanized processes to manufacture complicated timepiece movements. Within 30 years, LeCoultre had created more than 350 different timepiece calibers, of which 128 were equipped with chronograph functions and 99 with repeater mechanisms. From 1902 and for the next 30 years, LeCoultre produced most of the movement blanks for Patek Philippe of Geneva.

Jaeger-LeCoultre

In 1903, Parisian Edmond Jaeger challenged Jacques-David LeCoultre, grandson of Antoine, to manufacture ultra-thin calibers of his design. Out of their relationship emerged a collection of ultra-thin pocket watches, followed by others that eventually, in 1937, officially culminated in the Jaeger-LeCoultre brand. In 1907, French jeweler Cartier, a client of Jaeger's, signed a contract with the Parisian watchmaker under which all Jaeger's movement designs for a period of 15 years would be exclusive to Cartier. The movements were produced by LeCoultre. Also in 1907, the LeCoultre Caliber 145 set the record for the thinnest movement at 1.38 mm. JLC began manufacturing the Atmos clock in 1936 after purchasing the patent from Jean-Leon Reutter, who invented it in 1928. The company was officially renamed Jaeger-LeCoultre in 1937. In 1941, Jaeger-LeCoultre earned the highest distinction from the Neuchâtel Observatory for its tourbillon Caliber 170. In 1982, the Jaeger-LeCoultre museum was established in Le Sentier. In 2009, JLC produced the world's most complicated wristwatch, the Hybris Mechanica à Grande Sonnerie with 26 complications.

Other Products

Jaeger-LeCoultre has produced other measuring instruments, such as speedometers and fuel meters, under the Jaeger brand. The Jaeger instruments for automobiles were mostly used by the French automobile makers Citroën, Peugeot and Renault. Jaeger speedometers and tachometers were also supplied to British sports cars manufacturers such as Triumph. Many Italian cars such as Ferrari have used Jaeger automobile instrumentation.

LeCoultre in North America

Watches sold in North America were sold under the LeCoultre name from 1932 to approximately 1985. After that the Jaeger-LeCoultre name was adopted uniformly worldwide. According to factory records, the last movement to be used in an American LeCoultre watch shipped out of Le Sentier in 1976.

There is substantial confusion over the use of LeCoultre name for the North American market. Some collectors and misinformed dealers make the erroneous claim that the American LeCoultre has nothing to do with Jaeger-LeCoultre Switzerland. The confusion stems from the fact that, in the 1950s, the North American distributor of LeCoultre watches was the Longines-Wittnauer Group, which was also responsible for the distribution of Vacheron Constantin timepieces. Collectors have confused this distribution channel with the manufacture of the watches. Outside the actual distribution channel, the LeCoultre product, at the manufacturing level, had nothing to do with either Longines, Wittnauer or

Vacheron Constantin. In addition, the LeCoultre trademark was owned by the Société Anonyme de la Fabrique D'Horlogerie LeCoultre & Cie, Le Sentier. The LeCoultre trademark expired and was replaced by the Jaeger-LeCoultre trademark in 1985.

The Atmos Clock

Atmos is the brand name of a mechanical clock manufactured by Jaeger-LeCoultre, which does not need to be wound. It derives energy from small temperature changes and atmospheric pressure changes in the environment, and can run for years without human intervention.

The Atmos

The first Atmos clock was designed by Jean-Léon Reutter, an engineer in Neuchâtel, Switzerland, in 1928. This noncommercial prototype, which predated the Atmos name but is now known unofficially as Atmos 0, was driven by a mercury-in-glass expansion device. The mechanism operated on temperature changes alone. A one degree change in air pressure will wind an Atmos Clck for two days.

In 1929, Compagnie Générale de Radio (CGR) in France began manufacturing the first commercial model, Atmos 1, which used a mercury and ammonia bellows power source. In 1935, Jaeger-LeCoultre took over production of Atmos 1 while it developed a second design which used the present ethyl chloride power source. This model, later named the Atmos 2, was announced in 1936, but problems delayed full production until 1939. Subsequent models were based on this design. To date, over 500,000 Atmos clocks have been produced.

See also

- List of watch manufacturers

External links

- Official website [1]
- a (wmv) video presentation from JLC [2]
- History of Jaeger-LeCoultre [3]
- Photograph of Edmond Jaeger and Antoine LeCoultre [4]
- The history and calibers pictures of Jaeger-Lecoultre [5]

Ollech & Wajs

Ollech & Wajs

Ollech & Wajs (O&W) is a watch company based in Zurich, Switzerland.

History

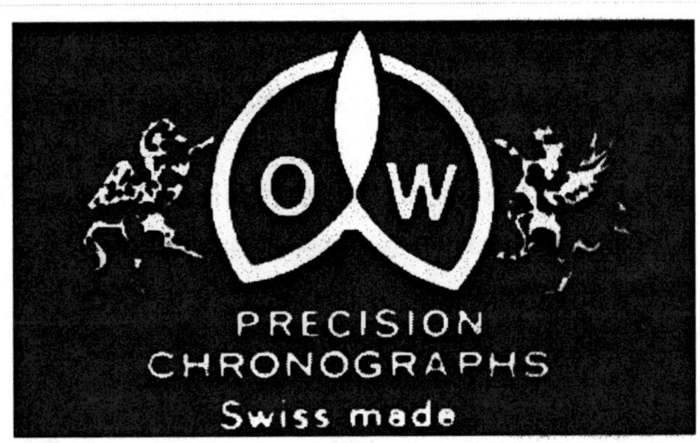

O&W logo

Ollech & Wajs started business in the 1950s when Albert Wajs began making and supplying stainless steel bracelets for wristwatches. In 1956, a partnership was formed with Joseph Ollech, and they soon began manufacturing wristwatches. Business was done from their retail premises in Zurich. They soon began to expand into world wide markets, more notably the US and UK markets by advertising in magazines that were popular with aviators, soldiers, divers and sportsmen, selling direct to the end user by mail order from Switzerland.

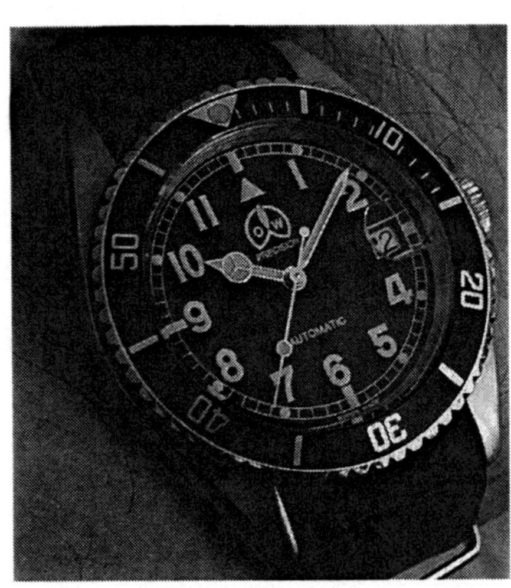
O&W M1 diver model

In the 1960s O&W sold a variety of professional automatic and manual-wind mechanical military and dive watches for an average of US $12. The Ollech & Wajs M 65 military watch was often sold at PX's on US military bases. These watches became very popular with US soldiers who bought them privately as a replacement for their government issued disposable watches. Sales reached an all time high during the Vietnam War era when they were selling thousands of watches via direct mail order. Towards the late 1970s, Mr. Wajs bought up much of the Breitling company's stock for the aviation models such as the *Navitimer*. They began producing their own label watches using Breitling cases and the same calibre movements used in Breitling watches. These watches were branded "Aviation" and are now prized amongst collectors. During the first season of the 1970s British television series The Professionals, actors Martin Shaw and Lewis Collins wore what appear to be Ollech & Wajs *Caribbean 1000* wristwatches.

Due to the growing popularity of quartz powered watch mechanisms in the late 1970s, much of the mechanical watchmaking industry suffered, and O&W finally ceased production in the early 1980s. In the 1990s, the company resumed production under a new company name, *A.I. Wajs*, formed by Albert Wajs. They continue to use the logo and the brand name Ollech & Wajs or O&W, as these brand names are owned by Albert Wajs.

See also

- Automatic watch
- Mechanical watch

External links

- O & W Watches home page [1]
- 1969 O&W catalog [2]

Hublot

Hublot

Type	Private (subsidiary of LVMH)
Industry	Watchmaking
Founded	1980
Headquarters	Nyon Switzerland
Key people	Carlo Crocco (founder) Jean-Claude Biver (CEO and minority shareholder since 2004)
Products	Wristwatches
Revenue	▲ CHF 250 million (2010)
Website	www.hublot.com [1]

Hublot is a Swiss enterprise creating luxury watches and founded in 1980 by Carlo Crocco. The company currently operates as a wholly-owned subsidiary of France's LVMH.

History

A scion of the Italian Binda Group dynasty, best known for making Breil watches, Carlo Crocco left the company in 1976 to strike out on his own and create a new watch company. Moving to Switzerland he formed MDM Geneve and set about designing a watch that he named the Hublot after the French word for "porthole". The watch that he created featured the first natural rubber strap in the history of watchmaking. It took 3 years of research to create the strap. Despite failing to attract a single potential customer on the first day of its debut at the 1980 Basel Watch Fair, the watch quickly proved to be a commercial success with sales in exces of $2m in its first year.

The Jean-Claude Biver era

Carlo Crocco, preoccupied by his own design work and many activities for the Hand-in-Hand Foundation, a charity helping deprived children all around the world, set out to look for the man who could oversee his watchmaking business. In late 2003, Jean-Claude Biver, then president of Swatch Group's Omega division, met Carlo Crocco, and in May 2004, Biver assumed duties as CEO, becoming a board member and minority shareholder in Hublot Watches.

Upon his arrival, Biver set about creating a new flagship collection that was unveiled in Basel in April 2005, with the Hublot "Big Bang" chronograph. It was an immediate success and orders increased threefold in one year. A few months later, in November 2005, the Big Bang chronograph was awarded internationally, receiving the "2005 Design Prize" in the "Geneva Watchmaking Grand Prix", the "Sports Watch Prize" at the "Watch of the Year" ceremony in Japan, and the Middle Eastern Prize for the "Best Oversized Watch" at the Editor's Choice "Watch of the Year" in Bahrain. Following the arrival of Biver in 2004, the brand's sales hit 24 million Swiss francs and by the end of 2006, sales were bordering on the 100 million Swiss franc mark.

Hublot stores

In February 2007, Hublot opened its first mono-brand store in Paris, in the Rue Saint-Honoré. The second was opened in the summer of that year, in the Hôtel Byblos, Saint-Tropez.

Acquisition by LVMH

In April 2008 it was announced that luxury goods group LVMH had acquired Hublot from founder Carlo Crocco for an undisclosed fee, adding to its existing portfolio of watch brands including TAG Heuer.

Hublot WiseKey

At BaselWorld 2009, Hublot unveiled a new method of detecting counterfeit watches. Using a WiseKey smart card, the system authenticates watches on Hublot's servers. The system went live in August of 2009.

Sponsorships

To increase the public profile of their brand Hublot have engaged in a number of sponsorship deals. In 2008, they agreed a sponsorship deal with the football club Manchester United, worth £4 million a year. That same year they provided special versions of their Big Bang watches to referees officiating at UEFA Euro 2008. In March 2010, Hublot was appointed the Official Watchmaker of Formula 1. In April 2010 Hublot became the official time keeper of the 2010 FIFA World Cup and the 2014 FIFA World Cup. They have also been involved in a tie-up with the Financial Times, sponsoring the newspaper's iPad app.

External links

- Brand's official website [2]
- HR Pictures [3]
- Collection novelties [4]

Eterna

Eterna

Type	Subsidiary of Porsche Design
Industry	Watch manufacturing
Founded	1856 by Josef Girard and Urs Schild
Headquarters	, Grenchen, Switzerland
Website	www.www.eterna.ch [1]

Eterna is a Swiss watch company founded in Grenchen, Canton Solothurn on the 7th of November 1856 by Dr Josef Girard and Urs Schild. They initially specialised in producing pocket watches with alarms. In 1906 the company name changed from U. Schild to Eterna. In 1908 they became the first company to produce an alarm wristwatch. The movement production part of the company eventually became ETA SA.

In 1995 Eterna was bought by the German company Porsche Design.

History

The basis of the Eterna Watch Company was founded in 1851. By the 1900s, wristwatches were just starting to become fashionable. Schild Fréres, as the company was then known, started to produce lady's wristwatches from adapted small pocket watches. In 1905, the company changed their name to Eterna. The company continued to be at the leading edge of watch developments, and in 1908 it patented the first alarm wristwatch. The watch went into production in 1914 and was launched at the Swiss National Exhibition at Berne in that year.

By 1932, Eterna had set up a subsidiary company, ETA, to make movements for itself and other Swiss watch companies. This same year Theodore retired and handed over the control of the company to his nephew Rudolf Schild. Although retired, Theodore remained on the board of directors until his death in 1950.

Eterna produced many innovations in their history, the smallest production wristwatch with a Baguette movement in 1930, an eight-day alarm watch in the 1930s and their first automatic watch in 1938.

Probably the most famous Eterna watch was their Eterna-matic. This watch was launched in 1948. The design of the automatic winding was one of Eterna's greatest designs. The weight ran on small ball bearings making it very efficient, hence the trademark of five ball bearings. The Eterna-matic continued in various styles and was still available in 1998, and has indeed been relaunched.

After 1982, the Eterna company was sold several times. By 1995, it ended up being owned by F.A.P. Beteiligungs GmbH. In 1999, Eterna produced a range of watches that were marketed under the Porsche Design label. The company is still at the forefront of modern wristwatch design.

External links

Official website [2]

Jovial (watch)

Jovial (watch)

Brand Jovial

Jovial is a Swiss manufacturer of watches, with headquarters in Biel, Switzerland. Formed in 1929, Mohamed Dabaan is the current CEO Jovial has its regional office in Dubai, UAE

Jovial has large presence in middle east and rapidly expanding worldwide. Jovial participates in international expo / exhibitions. Jovial uses ETA SA movements for some of their watches.

Jovial means a "reflection of joy and happiness".

See also

Jovial Montres SA Official Site [1]
Old Official Site [2]
International Watch Club [3]
Jovial 7000 Chronograph Series [4]
[Al Daba'an Trading Company]

Greubel Forsey

Greubel Forsey

GF GREUBEL FORSEY INVENTEURS HORLOGERS	
Type	Watch Maker
Industry	Watch Making
Founded	2004
Headquarters	La Chaux-de-Fonds, Switzerland
Area served	Worldwide
Key people	Robert Greubel and Stephen Forsey - Co-Founders. Emmanuel Vuille - CEO
Products	Luxury Timepieces
Website	www.greubelforsey.com [1]

Greubel Forsey is a watchmaking company specializing in very high-end complicated timepieces. It was launched in 2004 by *Robert Greubel* and *Stephen Forsey* and is based in La Chaux-de-Fonds, Switzerland.

It has made itself a name as a watch manufacturer, specially thanks to its invention of watches with two and four tourbillon mechanisms in the same watch case, and the patented mechanisms that allows them to get their force from the same main spring.

Corporate history

Robert Greubel and Stephen Forsey launched Greubel Forsey in 2004 at Baselworld with the introduction of their *Double Tourbillon 30° (DT30)*. Both men had been working together since 1992 at Renaud & Papi, where they developed complicated watch movements.

In 2006 the Richemont group acquired a 20% stake in Greubel Forsey's share capital.

In 2006 the company collaborated with American jeweller Harry Winston to make the *Opus 6* model.

The company has also invented and presented four different tourbillon-based watches: the *Double Tourbillon 30° (DT30°)* in 2004, the *Quadruple Tourbillon à Différentiel* in 2005, the *Tourbillon 24 Secondes Incliné* in 2006, and the *Invention Piece 1* in 2007, derived from the original DT30°.

EWT

The company presented in 2005 a proprietary development methodology called EWT (Experimental Watch Technology) to experiment, test and ratify their projects in-house. It's a proprietary research and development platform. It incorporates its own laboratory.

Two inventions current in EWT are the '*Binomial*', a mono-material balance-and-spring wheel combination mechanism using isochronically stable materials, and the "Différentiel d'Egalité", a constant force device based in a spherical differential. This differential keeps providing the same constant force to all the four tourbillons, solving the typical problem where the main spring gives different amount of force depending on how much potential energy it retains.

Founders

Robert Greubel grew up in Alsace/France and began his horological career by working with his watchmaker father in the family shop, Greubel Horlogerie. In 1987 Greubel moved to Switzerland to join IWC, where he helped develop their Grand Complication. In 1990 he joined Renaud & Papi SA (now Audemars Piguet Renaud & Papi SA) as a prototypist for complicated movements and rose to become managing director and partner.

Stephen Forsey grew up in St. Albans/England, where he was inspired by his father's passion for mechanics and engineering. From 1987 to 1992 Forsey specialized in antique clock restoration and became head of Watch Restoration at Asprey's in London. From 1988 to 1990 Forsey attended two five-month courses at the WOSTEP watchmaking school in Neuchâtel and in 1992 joined Robert Greubel's team at Renaud & Papi SA (now Audemars Piguet Renaud & Papi SA), developing complicated watch movements.

In 1999 both Greubel and Forsey began working independently, and in 2001 they founded together Complitime SA, a company specializing in created mechanisms with complicated movements for up-market watch brands.

At the world watch fair at BaselWorld in 2004, after many years in development, Robert Greubel and Stephen Forsey launched their first watch, the Double Tourbillion 30° (DT30°), under their own brand 'Greubel Forsey'.

Robert Greubel and Stephen Forsey are founding members of the Time aeon Foundation

Products

The company specializes in designing and manufacturing high-end watches based on the Tourbillon mechanism, with only a few tens of units manufactured every year, which are sold for hundreds of thousand of Swiss francs.

- *Double Tourbillon 30° (DT30°) Vision/Secret.*

This watch was presented in 2004 features one carriage which rotates once per minute and is inclined at 30°, inside another carriage which rotates every four minutes. The company claims rotating one Tourbillon inside another will average out errors on the balance induced by gravity. It is available in two versions, with the tourbillon mechanism either visible behind the dial or only through the back.

Double Tourbillon 30° 'Vision'. It was the first model launched by the company, featuring two tourbillon mechanism in one case.

- *Invention Piece 1 (IP1).*

Derived from the mechanism above *Invention Piece 1* has a modified appearance, with red and blue triangular 'hands' and a sub-second dial and a 'power reserve indicator' above and to the right. A large polished bridge supports the double tourbillon carriages. Presented in 2007.

- *Quadruple Tourbillon à Différentiel (QDT).*

Greubel Forsey's third watch, presented in 2005, uses two double-tourbillons working independently. The company claims this contributes to an extremely high accuracy for the timepiece. A spherical differential connects the four rotating carriages, distributing torque between two wheels rotating at different speeds. The carriages are visible on the dial side and through a window on the side of the watch.

- *Tourbillon 24 Secondes Incliné (T24Si).*

Presented in 2006, the tourbillon cage in this watch has a higher angular velocity, resulting in rapidly changing positions. An alluminium alloy and titanium are used for their strength and lightness. Avional for the pillars of the tourbillon cage, and titanium for the carriage bridges. The watch system incorporates 88 parts and weighs 0.39 grams.

External links

- Official website [2]
- Discussion forum [3]
- History of Greubel Forsey [4], by Foundation de la Haute Horlogerie
- Interview to Stephen Forsey [5], by Jack Forster
- Interview with Stephen Forsey [6], regarding the Richemont group stake
- Quadruple tourbillon [7], iW magazine, 2007-01-24
- Robert & Stephen biography [8], iW magazine
- Eric Pfanner (2005-12-05). "Swiss watches move up into high-end brackets" [9]. *International Herald Tribune*.
- Ian Skeller (August 2007). "Robert Greubel and Stephen Forsey: Inventors Inventing Inventions" [10]. Revolution magazine.

Gallet & Co.

Gallet & Co.

Type	Privately held company
Industry	watch movement & case manufacturing
Founded	1466 by Humbertus Gallet under family name (Geneva, Switzerland), later registered as Gallet & Cie in 1826 by Julien Gallet (La Chaux-de-Fonds, Switzerland)
Headquarters	Zollikon-Zürich, Switzerland
Key people	Georg Raytchev (Master Watchmaker) Walter Hediger (CEO) David R. Laurence (COO)
Products	wristwatches, stopwatches, and industrial timers for professional application
Website	Gallet Official Website [1]

Gallet is a historical manufacturer of high-end Swiss timepieces.

Gallet is the world's oldest watch and clock making house with history dating back to Humbertus Gallet, a clock maker who became a citizen of Geneva in 1466. The Gallet & Cie (Gallet & Company) name was officially registered by Julien Gallet (1806–1849) in 1826, who moved the family business from Geneva to La Chaux-de-Fonds, Switzerland. Prior to this date, operations commenced under the name of each of the family patriarchs.

Gallet is best known during the 20th century to the present day for its line of MultiChron chronograph wristwatches. Produced primarily for military, industrial, and other professional applications, Gallet's MultiChron watches often incorporated a number of advanced timekeeping innovations.

A Gallet timepiece of particular renown was the Flight Officer time zone chronograph. Commissioned by Senator Harry S. Truman in 1939 for pilots of the United States Army Air Forces, the Flight Officer (a.k.a. Flying Officer) had a rotating 12 hour bezel and the names of 48 major world cities printed on the periphery of the dial (face). These features made it possible to calculate changes in the time as an aviator flew across lines of longitude. Besides being the first time zone calculating wristwatch, the Flight Officer was one of the world's first wrist chronographs to be housed in a water resistant case. Truman wore a Gallet Flight Officer during his terms as 33rd president (1945–1953).

The modern Gallet Company is one of a small handful of independent Swiss watch brands that still maintain in-house manufacturing facilities. While recently expanding the company's marketing focus to reach a wider audience of "civilian" consumers for its expensive professional-use timepieces, Gallet continues to privately produce components and modules for a number of other entities within the luxury-class timekeeping industry.

History

For the Gallet family of watchmakers, the relocation to La Chaux-de-Fonds in 1826 after 350 years in Geneva proved to be a most advantageous move. With the resources available in the "Watch Valley", family patriarch Julien Gallet (1806–1849) was able to expand the new company's distribution of its pocket watches to all of Europe.

In 1855, Julien Gallet's son Léon (1832–1899) purchased Grumbach & Co., complete with factory and equipment, to facilitate the need for greater manufacturing capabilities. With this increase in work area, Gallet was able to bring together under one roof, many of the Jura Region's watchmakers to help meet Europe's increasing demand for watches.

Léon Gallet allowed his watchmakers to benefit through the registration of patents in their own names. This approach allowed the company to offer an extensive range of watches, and Gallet & Cie grew to become one the largest timekeeping entities in Switzerland.

Léon Gallet set his sights on the rest of the world markets. In 1864, Léon's brother, Lucien Gallet (1834–1879), established the company's first US location in Chicago, with a New York City office following soon after. Together with Jules Racine, a cousin of the Gallet brothers living in the US, the company began its expansion into the American market.

Due to the American consumer's preference for domestically styled products, the Gallet Company created numerous new lines to accommodate this. Not including watches privately labeled for established jewelry retailers, Gallet introduced thirty-seven new brands. While the names that appeared on the dials and the overall appearance and function of these watches were tailored to American tastes, all cases and movements continued to be produced in Gallet's La Chaux-Fonds workshop.

Each of the numerous brands were designed to target a different demographic. Lower priced watches were supplied to the average working man, as well as expensive high-grade and complicated timepieces in solid gold cases for the wealthy. Gallet's finest pocket watches, hand-built in the classic Swiss tradition and retaining the family flagship and Electa names, were always available. Although not initially successful, included with the company's American offerings in 1895 were the world's first wrist-worn watches produced for mass consumption. By the end of the 19th century, the Gallet family was manufacturing and selling over 100,000 timepieces per year.

When the worldwide economic downturn of the 1930s caused international trade to plunge by as much as two-thirds, it suddenly became unprofitable for the Gallet Company to continue production of many of its recently established brands. Gallet chose instead, to consolidate its efforts back into its primary area of expertise, that of the manufacture of high quality professional-use timepieces. Under the family name, the Gallet Company continued to flourish by providing hand-held timers and chronograph wristwatches to allied military and industrial clients during the years leading up to and through World War II. During this period, the Gallet's sales again surpassed 100,000 units annually.

A wartime Gallet timepiece of particular renown was the Flight Officer time-zone chronograph (1939–present). Commissioned by Senator Harry S. Truman's senatorial staff in 1939 for the United States Army Air Force, this wristwatch made it possible to calculate changes in the time as a pilot flew across lines of longitude.

After the war, Gallet's renewed worldwide popularity with civilians and professionals in the fields of aviation, sports, medicine, and technology eliminated the necessity to manufacture numerous secondary brands. With the exception of the few brand names that the company retained for its sports and industrial stopwatch lines, most of Gallet's previously held trademarks went back into circulation.

Time Line

- **1466** - Humbertus Gallet, living and working in Geneva, becomes a citizen of the republic on the 18th of April. Historical references point to his profession as a horloger or clock maker.
- **1685** – Due to the abolishment by French King Louis XIV of the tolerance agreement of Nantes, additional members of the Bourg-en-Bresse Gallet family, whose professions are documented as goldsmiths and watchmakers, join their relatives in Geneva to live and practice their trade.
- **1702** - Philippe Gallet ((1679–1739), son of Jacques Gallet (1649–1700) and Marie Bouvier Gallet, is included in the Geneva Registry of Jewelers and Watchmakers.
- **1742** - Pierre Gallet (1712–1768) marries noblewoman Jeanne Renée de Rabours. The marriage contract records Pierre Gallet's profession as master goldsmith. This document also lists the occupation of Pierre's father, Philippe Gallet (1679–1739), as goldsmith and watchmaker.
- **1744** - Jeanne Renee gives birth to a son, Jacques, who follows in his father's occupation as jeweler and watchmaker.
- **1774** - Jacques Gallet (1745–1806) fathers a son, Jean-Louis Gallet (1774–1809).
- **1804** - Napoleon annexes Geneva, naming it the Lemanique Republic. Jean Louis Gallet becomes a French citizen and continues his father's jewelry and watch making company until his pre-mature death in 1809 at age 35.
- **1826** - Julien Gallet (1806–1849), son of Jean Louis, relocates the family watch making business to La Chaux-de-Fonds, a major center for pocket watch production. At this time, the company is officially registered as Gallet & Cie (Gallet & Company), a break from the tradition of naming the business after the family patriarch.
- **1848** - Julien Gallet dies at 43, after which, the company is run by his widow Louise, and sons Leon and Lucien.

- **1855** - Léon Gallet (1832–1899) becomes the patriarchal figure of the rapidly growing Gallet & Cie. He expedites the expansion of the company and the need for more workshop space by acquiring Grumbach & Co., which produces watches with the brand name Electa. Gallet & Cie. is renamed Electa Gallet & Cie. and produces watches under both the Gallet and Electa brand names.
- **1864** - Léon Gallet's brother Lucien Gallet establishes the company's first US location in Chicago, with a New York City office following soon after. Together with Jules Racine, a cousin of the Gallet brothers living in the US, the company expands its distribution to the American market.
- **1876** - In response to competition for sales of timepieces in Europe by large American watch manufacturer's, Léon Gallet, together with Louis and Jules Courvoisier, Ernest Francillon of Longines, and Constant Girard-Gallet of Girard-Perregaux, found the "Intercantonal Company for Industrial Development of the Jura Industries". Benefiting from the unified strength of combined Swiss manufacturing resources, the group is able to maintain its sales dominance in Europe. Marketing for the syndicate is primarily European based with an emphasis on sales to England.
- **1880** - Henriette Gallet (1860–1939), daughter of Léon Gallet, is wed to Émile Courvoisier (1858–1937), son of Louis Courvoisier (1825–1885), at which time the working relationship between these two important La Chaux-de-Fonds watch manufacturers becomes familial.
- **1881** – Léon L. Gallet commissions and trademarks the Gallet Lyre Mark. The Lyre Mark is stamped on watch cases and movements manufactured in the La Chaux-de-Fonds workshop.
- **1882** - A strategic partnership is formed with Jules Jeanneret & Fils, to supply mechanisms for Gallet's professional use line of hand-held timers and pocket chronographs.
- **1883** - Léon hands over management of the Gallet company to his older son Julien (1862–1934), but continues to remain involved until his 1899 death in New York. The JG initials are added to the Gallet Lyre Mark and the company name is temporarily changed to Julien Gallet & Cie to reflect the older son's control of the business. Georges Gallet (1865–1946), Léon's younger son, assists his brother with the management of the company while working part-time at Courvoisier & Frères. By this time, the Gallet Company is producing more than 100,000 watches annually.
- **1893** - Berthe Courvoisier (1868–1936), daughter of Louis Philippe Courvoisier and an heir to the family watch company, is wed to Georges Gallet, son of Léon. Berthe Courvoisier and her brother Émile, together with Georges Gallet and his sister Henriette, continue to manage the Courvoisier Frères watch company. Georges Gallet assumes the role as co-director of the company.
- **1895** - Gallet introduces the first wrist-worn watches for mass consumption by men and women to the American market. These first "wristwatches" are immediately rejected due to public perception as being too unusual for women and too feminine for men. All unsold examples are soon returned to Switzerland for disassembly. In spite of initial resistance to this groundbreaking innovation, wristwatches are issued during WWI as a more useful way for soldiers to tell time in combat situations. As a result, this new concept gains acceptance, and is soon added to the offerings of numerous other watch companies.

- **1896** - Rail road pocket watches with chronometer grade movements with patented regulators are created by Gallet under the Interocean brand name and distributed by Timothy Eaton (T. Eaton Department Store) for railway use.
- **1896** - Gallet wins a silver medal at the Swiss National Exhibition in Geneva.
- **1899** - Upon his death, Léon Gallet bequeaths a sum of 43,000 Swiss Francs (today equivalent to approx. 1,000,000 US dollars) to the town of La Chaux-de-Fonds, of which 25,000 Swiss Francs is used for the construction of the Musée international d'horlogerie (International Museum of Watch Making). To assist the museum in building its initial collection of timepieces, Georges Gallet donates over 100 highly complex and valuable Gallet, Electa, and Courvoisier watches. Georges Gallet serves as director of the museum for the next twenty years.
- **1900** - Shortly after Léon Gallet's death, the company name is changed back to Gallet & Cie (Gallet & Co.).
- **1905** - Gallet wins a Diploma of Honor at the Liege Exhibition.
- **1906** - The company name "Gallet & Cie, Fabrique d'horlogerie Electa" is registered to reinforce Gallet's ownership and control of the Electa brand. Under the Electa name, Gallet produces its highest quality timepieces.
- **1911** - Henri Jeanneret-Brehm, a member of the esteemed Jeanneret family of St. Imier watchmakers, purchases the Magnenat-Lecoultre factory with financial assistance from the Gallet company.
- **1912** - Gallet creates the first wristwatch for mass distribution to include a full-sized constant seconds hand originating from the center of the dial (face). This innovation proved useful for timing tasks that emphasized seconds over minutes and hours, including the measuring of the human heart rate. Gallet's new "sweep second" wristwatches were issued to military nurses and medics during World War I.
- **1914** - Gallet wins the Grand Prize in the Chronometer category at the Swiss National Exhibition in Berne.
- **1915** - Gallet supplies hand held and cockpit mounted timers to the British Air Force during WW I. Movements are produced in Gallet's Electa workshop and marked with the Electa name.
- **1916** - Gallet supplies wrist-worn timers to the British armed forces during World War I. This early chronograph wristwatch was an obvious transitional timepiece. While technically refined and reduced in size from a traditional hand-held timer, it still retains the three-piece case, porcelain enamel dial, and center button crown of its larger predecessor.
- **1917** - Gallet wins the 1st place award for chronometer accuracy at the Canton Observatory in Neuchâtel.
- **1918** – Jeanneret-Brehm begins manufacturing under the company name Excelsior Park. Deriving the name from Jenneret-Brehm's previously registered "Excelsior" trademark, the English variation of the French word for "park" is utilized at the prompting of Gallet to support the collaborative efforts of the two companies in their marketing focus on the American consumer. The cooperative

relationship of Excelsior Park and Gallet leads to the development of a number of time recording mechanisms, including the calibre 40. These new chronograph movements are utilized almost exclusively in Gallet and Excelsior Park wristwatches, with a small number supplied to the Girard Perregaux and Zenith companies when production capabilities allowed.

- **1927** - Gallet introduces the "Regulator" and "Duo Dial" wristwatches for the medical and technical professions. The large-sized lower subsidiary seconds dial of the rectangular Duo-Dial and the predominant resetting sweep-second hand of the Regulator simplify the task of calculating a person's per-minute heart rate.
- **1929** - While Gallet develops viable markets for its new wristwatch innovations, the company is able to survive the Great Depression by supplying professional use "tool watches" to its military and industrial clients.
- **1935** - As World War II becomes imminent, Gallet begins production of wristwatches, boat clocks with 8-day movements, and military stopwatches for Great Britain, Canada, and the U.S.A. At the start of World War II, production again surpasses 100,000 watches annually.
- **1936** - Gallet introduces the first water resistant cases for protecting the delicate mechanism of chronograph wristwatches from the damaging effects of humidity. This new innovation become standard on many models in Gallet's "MultiChron" line of professional use timepieces, as well as the upcoming Flight Officer military issue pilot's watch.
- **1938** - Commissioned by Senator Harry S Truman staff for the pilots of the U.S. Army Air Forces, Gallet creates the Flight Officer chronograph. This wristwatch provides a combination of new innovations. Besides the ability to accurately record events ranging from 1/5th second to 30 minutes in duration, the rotating 12-hour bezel and dial (face) printed with the major cities gives pilots the ability to calculate changes in the time as lines of longitude are crossed. Truman wears a Gallet Flying Officer during his two terms as US president.
- **1939** - Gallet produces the Multichron Petite. The Petite is one of the first wrist chronographs engineered exclusively for enlisted women assigned to technical and scientific tasks during WWII. Powered by the 10 ligne Valjoux 69 movement, and measuring only 26.6mm in diameter, the MultiChron Petite becomes the smallest mechanical chronograph manufactured to date.
- **1946** - With the end of World War II, and the death of his father Georges, Léon Gallet assumes management of the Gallet Company. Only minor changes are needed to transform the appearance of Gallet's military style watches into trendy chronographs for sportsmen and civilian pilots.
- **1965** – Gallet introduces the Excel-O-Graph. This pilot's wristwatch features a rotating bezel with integrated slide rule for making navigational calculations during flight.
- **1970** - Asian manufacturers begin releasing electronic quartz regulated timepieces onto the world markets. By continuing to build mechanical timepieces for a clientele not influenced by changing fads and convention, Gallet survives the so called "quartz crisis".
- **1975** - Upon the death of Léon Gallet, sons Pierre and Bernard assume management of the company. They acquire the Racine Company, which has been struggling as a result of devaluation of

the U.S. dollar.

- **1983** - Excelsior Park closes its factory on 6 April due to the lack of family successors and a sizable decrease in orders of mechanical movements from its Gallet partner during the difficult "quartz crisis". To continue to support owners of Excelsior Park powered watches, Gallet acquires the balance of the company's remaining inventory and assets. An attempt in 1984 by the Flume Company of Germany to revitalize Excelsior Park name proves unsuccessful.
- **1984** – Wein Brothers, a Canadian distributor of timing instruments, contracts with the Gallet Company to manufacture rugged wristwatches for distribution to the US Government. To facilitate the initial transactions, the watch dials (faces) of these military specification watches are marked Marathon, a previously held Gallet trademark. Wein Brothers continues to distribute military timepieces and related products under the Marathon brand to the present day.
- **1990** - Gallet supplies 30,000 "Navigator" wristwatches to the Marathon Company for distribution to the U.S. military. Prior to Marathon's fulfillment of the contract, prototypes are arduously tested by the US Government to withstand the most adverse of circumstances. All examples exceed the military's strict requirements for sustaining accuracy and functionality during combat conditions.
- **1991** - Pierre Gallet retires from the company due to ill health. His brother Bernard assumes control of the company, which continues to focus on the manufacture of professional-use timepieces.
- **1996** – To facilitate expansion, Bernard Gallet enters into a partnership with B. Neresheimer Ltd., a company with over a hundred years experience in the manufacture and distribution of fine silver wares and high-end luxury goods.
- **2002** - The Gallet factory is relocated from La Chaux-de-Fonds to Grandson, a canton of Vaud approximately one hour from Geneva. Walter Hediger, a member of the Neresheimer family, takes the reins of Gallet as its CEO.
- **2004** - Company activity becomes concentrated near Zurich. Bernard Gallet remains active with the company until his death in 2006.
- **2008** - Gallet & Co co-sponsors "Time in Office" at the National Watch and Clock Museum, an exhibition of timepieces worn by America's presidents extending back to the pocket watches of George Washington. One of the featured items in the exhibit is the Gallet Flight Officer chronograph worn by Harry S Truman during his years in office as the 33rd president of the US.
- **2009** - Gallet & Co co-sponsors "Time & Exploration" at the National Watch and Clock Museum, an exhibit highlighting the importance of time and timekeeping in the fields of exploration and navigation.

Early Innovations

Among the Gallet's professional timekeeping innovations are:

- The first wristwatch with a center-originating sweep second hand for heart rate calculation (1912)
- The first wrist chronograph with a waterproof case (Gallet MultiChron, 1936)
- The first chronograph wristwatch with multiple time zone calculator (Gallet Flight Officer, 1938)
- The first miniature chronograph wristwatch for professional women (Gallet MultiChron Petite, 1939)
- The first chronograph wristwatch with additional 24 hour GMT hand (Gallet MultiChron Navigator GMT, 1945)
- The first 24 hour reading wrist chronograph (Gallet MultiChron 24, 1947)

Early Awards and Recognition

- 1896 Swiss National Exposition, Geneva — Silver Medal
- 1905 Universal Exposition of Liege — Grand Diploma of Honor
- 1914 Swiss National Exposition, Berne — Grand Prize in the Chronometer category
- 1917 Canton Observatory, Neuchâtel — 1st Place Award for Chronometer Accuracy

Gallet Brands/Trademarks (Pre-1940's)

- Breadfort Watch Co. (reg. pre-1898, pocket watches)
- Bridgeport Watch Co. (reg. 17 Dec 1886, pocket watches)
- Chancellor Watch (reg. pre-1898, pocket watches)
- Chief (reg. 28 Aug 1889, pocket watches)
- Commodore (reg. 7 May 1889, pocket watches)
- Continental Watch Co. (reg. 12 Aug 1879, complicated pocket watches)
- Defender (reg. pre-1895, pocket watches)
- Director Watch Co. (reg. pre-1895, pocket watches)
- Duchess (reg. pre-1898, woman's pocket watches)
- Electa & Cie. (extra high-grade & complicated pocket watches))
- Enterprise (reg. pre-1898, pocket watches)
- Eureka Time Keeper (reg. 14 Jan 1884, pocket watches)
- Favorite (reg. 16 Feb 1884, pocket watches)
- Galco (reg. 14 Mar 1925, Excelsior Park stopwatches)
- Gipsy (reg. pre-1895, woman's pocket watches)
- Governor (reg. pre-1898, rail road style pocket watches)
- Harlem Watch Co. (reg. pre-1898, pocket watches)
- Interocean (reg. 3 Jun 1910, Canadian Rail Road pocket watches)

- Jerome Park Watch Co. (reg. pre-1924, high grade pocket chronographs with Excelsior Park and Minerva movements)
- Jarco Watch (reg. pre-1898, pocket watches)
- Lady Racine (reg. 12 Aug 1879, lady's pocket watches)
- Lifetime Series (reg. 19 Oct 1914, high grade watches, produced in the Electa workshop for Macy's, New York)
- Lily (reg. 17 Jan 1881, lady's pocket watches)
- Majesty (reg. pre-1897, lady's pocket watches)
- Marathon (reg. 19 Oct 1915, pocket watches)
- Mars MultiChron Watch Co. (wrist chronographs)
- National Park (reg. 13 Jan 1891, Excelsior Park stopwatches & horse timers)
- Park Watch Company (reg. 21 Sep 1929, Excelsior Park stopwatches)
- Patriot Watch (reg. 16 Apr 1889, pocket watches)
- Railroad Watch (reg. 12 Aug 1879)
- Richmond (reg. 29 Aug 1889, pocket watches)
- Security (Excelsior Park stopwatches)
- Select (reg. pre-1898, Excelsior Park stopwatches)
- Success (reg. 13 Jan 1891, pocket watches)
- Trilby Watch (reg. pre-1895, pocket watches)
- Trotter (reg. pre-1897, Excelsior Park stopwatches & horse timers)
- Union Square (reg. 2 Oct 1883, pocket watches)
- Warrior Watch (reg. pre-1898, pocket watches)
- Wonder Watch (wrist chronographs)

Gallet Watch and Clock Making Dynasty

- **Humbertus Gallet** (1430–1492) clock maker, became a citizen of Geneva on 18 April 1466
- **Gonin Gallet** (1543–1610) grandson of Humbertus Gallet, clock maker, Geneva
- **Claude Gallet** (1605–1675) son of Gonin Gallet, watch and clock maker, Geneva
- **Jacques Gallet** (1649–1700) son of Claude Gallet, watchmaker and silk merchant, Geneva
- **Philippe Gallet** (1679–1739) son of Jacques Gallet, goldsmith & watchmaker, Geneva
- **Pierre Gallet** (1712–1768) son of Philippe Gallet, goldsmith & watchmaker, Geneva
- **Jeremie Gallet** (1729–1763) son of Pierre Gallet, watchmaker, apprenticed under Benedict de Rabours in 1745, Geneva
- **Jacques Gallet** (1745–1806) son of Pierre Gallet, goldsmith, watch & case maker, Geneva
- **Jean-Louis Gallet** (1774–1809) son of Jacques Gallet, goldsmith, watchmaker, watch case maker, Geneva

- **Julien Gallet** (1806–1849) son of Jean-Louis Gallet, watch & case maker, registered family business in La Chaux de Fonds as Gallet & Cie.
- **Louise Gallet** (1808–1865) widow of Julien Gallet, ran the company after her husband's death
- **Léon L. Gallet** (1832–1899) son of Julien Gallet, watchmaker, La Chaux de Fonds
- **Lucien F. Gallet** (1834–1879) son of Julien Gallet, watchmaker, La Chaux de Fonds & Geneva
- **Julien Gallet** (1862–1934) son of Leon L. Gallet, watchmaker, La Chaux de Fonds
- **Georges Gallet** (1865–1946) son of Leon L. Gallet, watchmaker, La Chaux de Fonds (together with wife Berthe Courvoisier Gallet and brother-in-law Émile Courvoisier, controlled the Courvoisier Frères watch company)
- **Léon Gallet** (1899–1975) son of Georges Gallet, watchmaker, La Chaux de Fonds
- **Pierre Gallet** (1926–1995) son of Leon Gallet, watchmaker, La Chaux de Fonds
- **Bernard L. Gallet** (1930–2006) son of Leon Gallet, watchmaker, La Chaux de Fonds

Wrist Watch Models - 1900 to the Present

- **Excel-O-Graph** – pilot's navigational chronograph with rotating slide rule bezel
- **Flying Officer** (a.k.a. Flight Officer in US & canada) - pilot's chronograph with world time zone calculator
- **Marathon Navigator** – water resistant antimagnetic pilot's watch with rotating 12 hour bezel
- **MultiChron 12** - professional chronograph with 12 hour recording capabilities
- **MultiChron 30** - professional chronograph with 30 minute recording capabilities
- **MultiChron 45** - professional chronograph with 45 minute recording capabilities
- **MultiChron Astronomic** - 12 hour chronograph with triple date and moon phase
- **MultiChron Calendar** - professional chronograph with accurate day, date, and month functions
- **MultiChron Commander** - mid-size chronograph for both men and women professionals
- **MultiChron Decimal** - professional chronograph for technical & scientific use
- **MultiChron Diver** - professional scuba diver's chronograph with rotating 60 minute bezel
- **MultiChron Navigator GMT** - professional chronograph with additional 24 GMT hour hand
- **MultiChron Officer** - small size square dress or formal chronograph for officers
- **MultiChron Petite** - miniature chronograph for professional and enlisted women
- **MultiChron Pilot** - pilot's chronograph with rotating time zone bezel
- **MultiChron Pilot Petite** - miniature chronograph with time zone bezel for women pilots
- **MultiChron Rattrapante** - chronograph with simultaneous dual function recording
- **MultiChron Regulator** - professional chronograph with offset minute and hour dial
- **MultiChron Yachting** - professional chronograph with regatta countdown timer

Vintage Wrist Watch Gallery

Historic Timer Gallery

Bibliography

- Brunner, Gisbert L.; Pfeiffer-Belli, Christian (1999), *Wristwatches Armbandhuren Montres-bracelets*, Germany: Konemann, ISBN 3-8290-0660-8.
- Lang, Gerd R.; Meis, Reinhard (1993), *Chronograph Wristwatches To Stop Time*, Germany: Schiffer, ISBN 0-88740-502-9.
- Cardinal, Catherine; Piquet, Jean-Michel (2002), *Musée International d'Horlogerie, Catalogue of Selected Pieces*, Switzerland: Institut l'homme et le temps, ISBN 2-940088-10-1.
- Whitney, Marvin E. (1992), *Military Timepieces*, USA: American Watchmakers Institute Press, ISBN 0-918845-14-9.
- Trueb, Lucien F. (2008), *Children of the Quartz Revolution, Institut l'homme et le temps, Musée International d'Horlogerie, La Chaux-de-Fonds*, Switzerland: Athena, ISBN 978-2-940088-25-6.

External links

- Official Gallet Website [2]
- National Watch and Clock Museum [3]
- Musée International d'Horlogerie [4]

Wyler (company)

Wyler (company)

Wyler is a Swiss watch manufacturer

Paul Wyler was born in 1896.

Wyler presented its first 16 and 19-line precision movements to the public in 1927. The particularity of these was the Incaflex balance wheel, which was legendary at the time. The Wyler Incaflex balance wheel is protected along its diameter by two curved, elastic arms, which absorb any shocks to the balance wheel. In addition to producing his own calibres, Wyler also modified movements of other large-scale producers and sold these on to other watch companies. In some cases, the basic calibre was changed so much that the movements should actually be considered as Wyler calibres.

In 1934, Wyler was the official watch of Italy's World Cup winning team.

In 1937 the company caused a stir by launching a water-resistant watch that was not fitted with the conventional soft gaskets. The mineral glass was pressed in between the edge of the case and a pressed or screwed bezel, the gap between the winding shaft and the watch case was sealed hydraulically by fitting the winding shaft and bushing together, in the same material, to 1/500mm.

Wyler gained worldwide notoriety with a spectacular marketing stunt in 1956, when two watches were dropped from the top of the Eiffel Tower and continued to function after the fall.

In 1960 manual and self-winding models from the Incaflex range became the official railway watch of the Santa Fe Railroad. In 1972, the Wyler Watch Corp. New York became a distributor for Eterna.

The rebirth of the brand

The brand was reborn as **Wyler Genève** at Baselworld 2006, following a decision by the Binda Group to reposition it.

At Baselworld 2007, the Wyler Genève Chronograph and tourbillons were presented, and in autumn 2007 the Wyler-Zagato watch was launched in conjunction with the Italian Atelier Zagato. The watch has an 8-day manual-winding manufacture movement.

Armand Nicolet

Armand Nicolet

Armand Nicolet is an exceptional quality Swiss watch manufacturer located in Tramelan, a mountain village in the Bernese Jura. Its history dates to its foundation in 1910 by Armand Nicolet the young watchmaker.

External links

- Armand Nicolet homepage [1]

Sandoz watches

Sandoz watches

Sandoz is a Swiss watch brand, originally established in the late 19th century by Henri Sandoz near Tavannes, Switzerland. There are now many variations of the Sandoz name which are used by at least four different companies around the world.

History

Henri Frédéric Sandoz (sometimes Frédéric Henri Sandoz), born in 1851, was a self-made man of Le Locle who in the 1870s founded Henri Sandoz & Cie., later producing complicated watches under the name of Cyma. In 1890, in partnership with two families named Schwob, Sandoz established a watch-making firm at Malleray, near Tavannes, in the French-speaking Bernese Jura of Switzerland. Their new business was known as Tavannes Watch Co. By the time of the death of Sandoz on 18 March 1913, many watches were made under the name of Henri Sandoz & Fils. The enterprise occupied a 'model factory' employing one thousand workers and producing 2,500 watches a day. Sandoz was reported to have a paternalistic policy towards his workforce, exercising a fierce social control.

Other names used by the Tavannes company at various times include Tavannes-Cyma, Bijou Watch Co., Tacy Watch Co., and Lisca. After the death of Sandoz, the company he founded went on growing. By 1938, it was manufacturing four thousand items a day.

Present day

Since 1971 the Sandoz brand name has been split into four main areas of production, due to its licences being leased or sold. This has led to four separate brands, Sandoz Singapore, Sandoz Hong Kong, Sandoz Swiss, and Sandoz Spain (Munreco). All of these produce watches under the Sandoz name, but each production company has its own line of products. Sandoz Swiss manufactures high quality watches, while Sandoz Hong Kong and Sandoz Singapore manufacture cheaper watches of lower quality. Sandoz Hong Kong products are assembled in Hong Kong using Swiss movements from ETA SA.

See also

- List of watch manufacturers

External links

- Gary M. Frazier, A Review of the Sandoz Explorer III, The Rolex That Never Was [1] at manthanein.com

Mido (watch)

Mido (watch)

Type	Member of the Swatch group
Industry	Watch manufacturing
Founded	1918 by George G. Schaeren
Headquarters	Le Locle, Switzerland
Key people	François Thiébaud, President
Products	Wristwatches
Parent	Swatch group
Website	www.mido.ch [1]

Mido is a Swiss watchmaker company founded in 1918.

History

Mido was founded in 1918 by George G. Schaeren in Biel, Switzerland. *Mido* is a Latin term that means "measuring".

Mido created one of the first self-winding (automatic) wristwatch in 1934 with the introduction of the Multifort. The Multifort was also noted for being shock resistant, water resistant and anti magnetic. In the 1940s Mido introduced the first center chronograph (a watch with all hands arranged in the center).

Today, Mido is a part of the Swatch Group, headquartered in Le Locle, Switzerland.

External links

- Official website [2]
- The Swatch Group [3]

References

Kathleen H. Pritchard: Swiss Timepiece Makers, 1775-1975: Phoenix Publishing; 1997.

Mb-microtec

mb-microtec

Type	Private
Industry	Military equipment
Founded	1968
Founder(s)	Walter Merz and Albert Benteli
Headquarters	Niederwangen, Switzerland
Products	Tritium lighted watches, maps readers
Website	www.mbmicrotec.com [1]

mb-microtec AG is a Swiss company primarily known for its watches that use tritium to illuminate the hands and numerals.

Established in 1918 by two chemists, Walter Merz and Albert Benteli, Merz & Benteli AG had split to create mb-microtec AG in 1968. Before then, the production of luminous colors were mainly supplied to Swiss watch making industries, and even to renowned scientists such as Marie Curie. The usage of tritium rather than glow paint was put into consideration for producing military-certified watches under the subsidy *traser*, and various other military components under *glotac*.

Roamer (watchmaker)

Roamer (watchmaker)

Type	Private
Industry	Watch manufacturing
Founded	1888
Founder(s)	Fritz Meyer
Headquarters	Solothurn, Switzerland
Products	Watches
Website	http://www.roamer.ch

Roamer is a Swiss watch manufacturer.

History

Roamer was founded in Solothurn, Switzerland, in 1888 by Fritz Meyer. At first, Meyer and employees concentrated on manufacturing cylinder escapements, and from 1904, when Meyer joined forces with fellow watchmaker Johann Studeli, watch movements. "Meyer & Studeli" (MST) units became a reputable brand before World War I. By 1923, production grew to one million units. In 1940 the company started its own dial production line. In 1945, a representative office opened in New York City. In 1952 Roamer Watches officially changed its name to Roamer Watch Co. SA. In 1955, Roamer patented an original Anfibio watertight watch case, which proved to be a commercial success. In 1972, the company launched its first quartz movement.

In 2003 Roamer returned to manufacturing of mechanical watches. Currently, it remains an independent watchmaking company, selling its products to over 70 countries. Roamer Watch Co. is a member of Federation of the Swiss Watch Industry FH.

Product lines

- Competence
- R-Line
- Stingray
- Classic
- Dreamline
- Superslender
- Ceramic

Sources

- http://www.roamer.ch
- http://www.watchcarefully.com/articles/roamer.html
- http://www.internationalwatchclub.com/roamer-watches/
- http://www.artistsguilds.com/watches/Roamer.htm
- http://www.fhs.jp/News/Roamer/RoamerE.htm (Federation of the Swiss Watch Industry)

Société Suisse pour l'Industrie Horlogère

Société Suisse pour l'Industrie Horlogère

Société Suisse pour l'Industrie Horlogère was the second most important Swiss Watch Group, holding Omega and Tissot.

It was created on February 24, 1930 in Geneva by Tissot et Omega, to be joined as from 1932 by Lemania Watch Co & A. Lugrin Co in L'Orient (Vallée de Joux) specialised in the manufacture of complications horlogères , enabling **Omega** to obtain the timing of the Summer Olympic Games 1932 in Los Angeles. This was an important step for the development of Omega's important Sports' Watches segment with exclusive chronographs, e.g. the famous Omega Speedmaster Professional **Moon watch**.

The Agreement foresaw Omega's concentration to the Luxury watches segment, whereas Tissot's mission was to concentrate on the medium price range segment

In 1983, SSIH and the Allgemeine Gesellschaft der schweizerischen Uhrenindustrie AG (ASUAG) the other most important Swiss Watch Group, were forced by their Swiss Banks to merge into a new holding company named Société de Microélectronique et d'Horlogerie (SMH), which has now been renamed the Swatch Group. (See [1]).

Dr Ernst Thomke was its first CEO until 1991. He instigated a total overhaul of both Omega and Tissot line of products, positioning both brands successfully back into the world markets.

External links

- Speedmaster [3]

Allgemeine Gesellschaft der schweizerischen Uhrenindustrie AG

Allgemeine Gesellschaft der schweizerischen Uhrenindustrie AG

Allgemeine Schweizerische Uhrenindustrie AG (ASUAG) (in French Société générale de l'industrie horlogère suisse SA) is the former biggest Swiss Watch Industry Group that had been created with the assistance of the Swiss Government and the Swiss Banks, as an answer to the crisis called upon by the Big Depression, in 1931.

1983, « ASUAG » and (SSIH), then the second most important holding company with Omega and Tissot were forced by the Swiss Banks to merge into Société de Microélectronique et d'Horlogerie (SMH), which now has been renamed Swatch Group (see [13]) ASUAG grouped most of the movement parts & Ebauches manufacturers on one side, and through its sub holding General Watch Co (GWC); many watch brands on the other side. Most of those companies are still being active, integrated into the new conglomerate.

During the years of crisis, since 1978 until 1991, Dr. Ernst Thomke was at the helm of the restructurations, firstly as CEO of ETA SA, then Ebauches SA, including a mandate as Administrator of ASUAG, and became SMH's first CEO in 1983, position that he held until 1991. At that time newly elected President and main shareholder Nicolas G. Hayek had already become the only person of reference.

External links

- [1] History of the creation of ASUAG through the association of the Ebauches companies
- [2] Free English translation
- [13] History of the Swatch Group
- [3] Swatch Group Official History

General Watch Co

General Watch Co

General Watch Co. (**GWC**) was the watch companies Holding of ASUAG.

History

ASUAG had been founded in 1931, with the assistance of the Swiss Government and the Swiss Banks, to combat the severe economic crisis and ensuing unemployment by means of refinancing (thus eliminate the deadly "dumping for survival" murderous competition witihin the still somewhat "cottage industry"-like status of a majority of the movements and parts thereof supplying companies) and complementary research and development programs in their respective companies.

Its mandate was to maintain, improve and develop the Swiss watch industry.

ASUAG also expanded gradually through the purchase of

- further Ebauches manufactures (movement blanks)
- movement parts manufactures (e.g. balance wheels, assortments, rubies) and
- a number of assemblers and manufacturers of complete watches, that were subsequently brought together under the subsidiary "GWC General Watch Co. Ltd."] "Manufacturing time", by Amy Glasmeier]:

Afiliated Watch Brands & Companies

- A. Reymond S.A. (Brands: Arsa, Damas and Hoga)
- Atlantic S.A
- Certina
- Diantus
- Edox
- Endura
- Eterna
- Hamilton
- Longines
- Microma
- Mido
- Oris

- Rado
- Roamer
- Rotary
- Technos

Merger with SSIH into SMH

However, it proved difficult to implement a common industrial policy for the subsidiaries concerned. Following repeated crises in the Swiss watch industry, by the 1970s, ASUAG (SSIH as well) were once again in trouble. Foreign competition, in particular the Japanese watch industry, with its mass production of cheap new electronic products and new technology, was rapidly establishing a strong foothold in the market.

Eventually, both ASUAG and SSIH faced liquidation: thus, in 1983, "GWC General Watch Co.", and its affiliated watch brands and factories, were merged with its parent company ASUAG, together with SSIH, into what has now become the Swatch Group, (see: [10] Swatch Group Official History Profile), under the patronage of the Swiss Banks that were at the time financially involved.

Spin Off

Some companies had however beforehand made themselves again independent or having been sold off, e.g.

- A. Reymond S.A. August Raymond official website [1]
- Atlantic S.A Atlantic official website [2]
- Edox Edox official website [3]
- Eterna Eterna official website [4]
- Oris Oris official website [5]
- Rotary Rotary Official website [6]
- Technos Technos official website [7]

Société de Microélectronique et d'Horlogerie

Société de Microélectronique et d'Horlogerie

Société de Microélectronique et d'Horlogerie was the original name of the new holding company issued from the merger enforced by the Swiss Banks in 1983 of both the SSIH and ASUAG, now Swatch Group (see [13]).

Dr. Ernst Thomke, previously CEO of Ebauches SA and ETA SA was appointed to head the newly established conglomerate as it first CEO. He held his position until 1991. When he resigned, its newly elected President of the Board, Nicolas G. Hayek, had already managed to become the only person of reference.

Endura Watch Factory

Endura Watch Factory

Endura S.A. is Swiss watch manufacturer founded in 1966 by General Watch Company (GWC) in Biel/Bienne, Switzerland, for the purpose of manufacturing watches under "private label". This company was also part of the merger between ASUAG and SSIH into SMH, now the Swatch Group. Now attached to ETA SA Manufacture horlogère Suisse, Endura SA is the Private Label and licensing division of the Swatch Group.

References

- [1] Swatch Group website's Endura page

External links

- [2] Endura Website

TechnoMarine

TechnoMarine

Industry	Jewellers
Founded	1997, in Geneva, Switzerland
Headquarters	Geneva, Switzerland
Products	Jewelry
Website	www.technomarine.com [1]

TechnoMarine was founded in 1997, by French entrepreneur Franck Dubarry, with the launch of the "Raft", a chronograph on a transparent plastic strap, selling 50,000 models in its first year and creating an entirely new category of luxury fashion timepieces, one which triggered a revolution in the luxury watch industry. Initially conceived as a "vacation souvenir watch", the "Raft" paved the way for a new generation of fine timepieces. </ref>

References

Techno Marine [1] Resource Site - http://techno-marine.net

West End Watch Co

West End Watch Co

Type	Private company
Industry	Watch manufacturing
Founded	1886 (by Arnold Amstutz and Constant Droz)
Headquarters	Leytron (Wallis), Switzerland
Key people	Jérôme Monnat Jr., current CEO
Products	Automatic and quartz wristwatches
Website	www.westendwatchco.ch [1]

West End Watch Company headquarters

West End Watch Company is a manufacturer of watches located at Leytron (Switzerland). It is one of the oldest Swiss brands and has been in business for more than 120 years.

The company has produced and distributed more than 15 million watches worldwide since 1886.

History

The West End Watch Company was created in 1886. The West End, a district of the centre of London, inspired its name to Mr. Arnold Charpié who was the Bombay representative of the Alcide Droz & Sons firm, a watch company established at Saint-Imier (Canton of Bern) in Switzerland.

In 1886, MM. Amstutz and Droz, the owner of Alcide Droz & Sons firm, began the exploitation of the trademark West End Watch Company in the Indian market and developed the first waterproof pocket watch ever produced : "L'Impermeable" (nowadays displayed at the International Watchmaking Museum of La Chaux-de-Fonds).

During the First World War, a large force of British and Indian soldiers was sent from Bombay to the Persian Gulf to reach Mesopotamia (modern-day Iraq). They received some West End Watch Company watches.

In 1917, West End Watch Company changed its name to Société des Montres West End SA and was registered in Geneva. At the same time the sub-brand *Sowar* was also registered.

In 1934, the Société des Montres West End SA was the first brand to introduce the Incabloc anti-shock system invented by Mr. Braunschweig.

In 1973, after several years of development, the company was finally sold, for lack of heirs, to his main supplier : "Aubry Brothers Ltd", established in Noirmont (Jura) to keep open the Bombay West End Watch Company's office.

Since 2000 the workshops and the head office of the company have been moved to Leytron, in Wallis. At the same time, the company was taken over by new shareholders and the management changed.

In 2005 West End Watch Company celebrated its 120th anniversary of uninterrupted presence in Asia with the introduction of its "Silk Road concept". This concept came from the fact that the Silk Road crossed most of the regions where the brand possessed, and still possesses, counters.

Nowadays, West End Watch Company is active in Saudi Arabia, in the United Arab Emirates, in the Himalaya Range (in particular in Nepal and in Bhutan) and as well as in western half of China.

2010 A first in the brand's history, West End Watch Company watches are now exclusively distributed/sold in the USA and Canada by Empire Brands. EB is a distributor of leading products around the globe.

In 2011, West End Watch Company will celebrate its 125 years of uninterrupted activity so a commemorative book redrawing the history of the brand will be published in 2010 in association with the Centre Jurassien d'Archives et de Recherches Economiques.

The model still manufactured today is *Sowar*. In Hindustani, *Sowar* means "warrior" and this name was selected in honor of Sir Thomas Edward Lawrence (Lawrence of Arabia) because it's said that he and his soldiers wore some West End Watch Company watches during the war.

Articles

- Ella Maillart mentions the presence of West End Watch Company watches in Western China in the 1930s in her book "Forbidden Journey - From Peking to Cashmir" (on page 252) : *He introduces us a robust Turki with blond beard whose 'West End Watch chronometer' features an inscription in which Aurel Stein expresses his thanks to Musa Ahoun, his interpret.*

External links

- Federation of the Swiss Watch Industry [2]
- Société des Montres WEST END SA [1]
- International Watchmaking Museum [3]
- http://www.westendwatchusa.com

Romain Gauthier

Romain Gauthier

Romain Gauthier is a manufacturer of watches.

Sources

- Underthedial [1]
- Journal Haute Horlogerie [2]
- Luxury Insider [3]

External links

- Official website [4]

Zodiac Watches

Zodiac Watches

Industry	Watch movement & case manufacturing
Founded	1882
Defunct	2001
Headquarters	Le Locle, Switzerland
Products	Wristwatches, accessories

Zodiac Watches is a brand of watches manufactured by Fossil, Inc.. Prior to the acquisition by Fossil in 2001, Zodiac SA was a Swiss manufacturer of high quality wristwatches.

History

In 1882, Ariste Calame founded a workshop for the production of special watches in Le Locle, Switzerland. The original name of the company was Ariste Calame and would later become Zodiac. The name "Zodiac" was used early but was not registered until 1908. The founder's son, Louis Ariste Calame, was sent to watchmaking school and then began to participate in the business in 1895 and took over the business that year.

The first flat pocket watch was launched to the public in 1928 and used the unique Zodiac calibre 1617 movement. In 1930, the brand designed and produced the first automatic sports watch and then produced the popular Zodiac Autographic. The Autographic was self-winding with a power reserve gauge, an unbreakable crystal, a radium dial, and was also water and shock resistant. The Autographic soon became the official watch of the Swiss Federal Railways.

In 1953 Zodiac launched the Sea Wolf. The Sea Wolf model was one of the first serious diver's watches manufactured and marketed to the masses. Later on Zodiac launched the Super Sea Wolf. The patented crown/stem system and improved case back design increased the water pressure rating to 750 meters.

"Zodiac killer"

The Zodiac watch cross-circle symbol was the same symbol used by a serial killer who operated in Northern California in the late 1960s. The Zodiac killer coined his name in a series of taunting letters he sent to the press which he signed using the Zodiac watch symbol. Zodiac suspect Arthur Leigh Allen wore a Zodiac Sea Wolf, which was a popular US Navy Seal watch at the time.

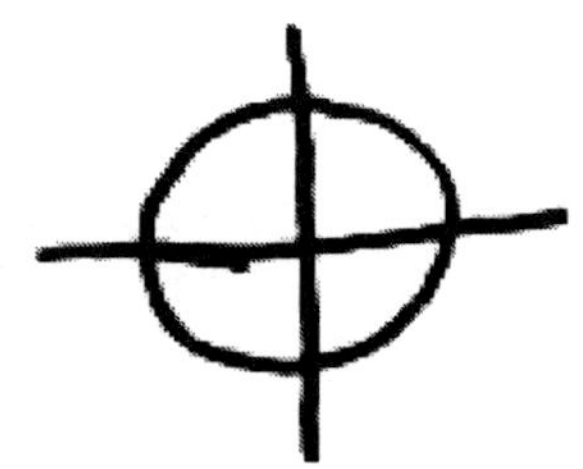

The symbol used by the Zodiac Killer to sign his correspondence

Financial troubles and the Fossil Inc. acquisition

In 1990 Willy Gad Monnier, formerly of Tag Heuer purchased the Zodiac brand, however this company, Montres Zodiac SA, went bankrupt in November 1997. In September 1998 Genender International, Inc. purchased the Zodiac inventory including their trademarks and registrations and other assets. Genender discontinued all of the "Point" series models, the Swiss Formulas, the Sea Wolf, and most automatic watches and all of the Zodiac automatic chronographs. The only two 1990's models kept were the Super Sea Wolf and the Marine Life, both of which were updated with new metal bands.

On October 1, 2001 Fossil Inc. acquired the worldwide rights to the Zodiac brand name for approximately 4.7 million for use in connection with watches, clocks and other timekeeping devices. In April 2002, the new Zodiac line was introduced at the Basel Watch Show in Switzerland, with the notable absence of any Sea Wolf model for the first time in 50 years.

External links

- Official website [1]
- Vintage Zodiacs [2]

Mathey-Tissot

Mathey-Tissot

Mathey-Tissot is a Swiss watch maker of prestige watches, originally established in the late 19th century by Edmond Mathey-Tissot at Les Ponts-de-Martel in the canton of Neuchâtel in Switzerland. It should not be confused with Tissot, a completely separate Swiss watchmaking firm established by Charles-Felicien Tissot.

Mathey-Tissot gold minute-repeater pocket watch, c. 1909

History

Edmond Mathey-Tissot established his watchmaking business at the village of Les Ponts-de-Martel in 1886. He began by specializing in complications, and especially repeater pocket watches, that is, watches which chime the minute and/or the hour and quarter-hour. The firm soon proceeded to make chronographs and won a number of prizes.

Mathey-Tissot 'Calamatic' gold triple calendar moon phase watch, c. 1947

In 1899, the outbreak of the Second Boer War led to such an expansion in demand for Mathey-Tissot watches that a new factory was built. Among the orders received was one from a nobleman in Scotland who commissioned 2,500 watches, having decided to present every man in his son's regiment with a repeater watch: in gold for officers, silver for other ranks.

In 1914, Mathey-Tissot was represented at the Kew Observatory Competition by six Observatory Chronometers capable of split-second timing, all six being rated 'Class A' with the comment 'specially good'. The same year, Mathey-Tissot gained the Grand Prix at the Swiss National Exhibition. During the First World War, the company supplied the United States Army's Corps of Engineers with precision chronographs in large quantities, while General Pershing, commanding the United States Expeditionary Force, chose the watch to award to members of his own staff. Both before and after the Second World War, the company continued to supply the U. S.

Army and the Royal Navy.

The name 'E. Mathey-Tissot & Co.' was protected by trademark in the United States in 1937.

The firm at one time had good relations with China and made watches of Chinese designs for that market which have been described as "complicated and painstaking pieces... in the realm of superior watchmaking".

In 1969 and 1970, Elvis Presley bought several dozen customized Mathey-Tissot automatic watches for giving to family, friends, and staff, the purpose being to identify the wearers as having a privileged right of access to Presley's concerts and tours. For this object, a bezel setting was created with the name ELVIS PRESLEY in raised letters and four stars.

Present-day

Mathey-Tissot today continues to make and customize watches with both mechanical and quartz movements. The company's logo is similar to the symbol of the British Campaign for Nuclear Disarmament, but turned upside-down, with the words *Mathey-Tissot* in manuscript, above the printed words "since 1886".

The name of Mathey-Tissot is registered with the World Intellectual Property Organization, under the company name E. Mathey-Tissot & Co SA, of Boulevard de Pérolle, Fribourg, Switzerland.

See also

- List of watch manufactures
- Manufacture d'horlogerie
- Federation of the Swiss Watch Industry FH

External links

- Mathey-Tissot - Les artisants du temps [1] - official web site
- Mathey-Tissot [2] at swiss-made-watches.com
- Elvis Presley watch by Mathey-Tissot, 1969 [3] (illustrated)

Blanchet (watch)

Blanchet (watch)

BLANCHET	
Industry	Watch manufacturing
Founded	1819
Founder(s)	Jean Blanchet (watchmaker)
Headquarters	, Switzerland
Products	Wristwatches, accessories
Owner(s)	D Group
Website	www.blanchetwatches.com/ [1]

Blanchet is an historic watch brand stated in Switzerland in 1819 by Jean Blanchet. The current owner of Blanchet is the D Group, that in 2010 relaunched the brand.

History

Jean Blanchet was a swiss watchmaker who grew up in France (Lyon) where his father Pierre Blanchet owned a small watch dial factory. Since youth, Jean Blanchet was fascinated by the French and Swiss watches tradition. He launch his own watch manufacturing in 1789. From the first steps his company had a cross-border success all over the old continent.

In 1828 Jean Blanchet married Laura Wilson, the daughter of an English ambassador. One year later she gave birth to their son Yves Blanchet.

In the age of 20 he decided to go to the Royal School of watchmaking (Ecole Royale de l'Horlogerie de Cluses).

Yves took over the company in 1852, when Jean died during an accident. Four years later he moved close to the Lake of Geneva, in Coppet, to perfection his watchmaking technique and start his own business "Manufacture d'Horologerie Blanchet & Cie".

Jean Blanchet owned some vineyards in Hight Savoye (Haute Savoie) near Geneva. He usually used to say "...designing and create a watch is similar to cultivate a vineyard..."

Famous Blanchet owners

Among the admirers of Blanchet watches there were some important historical figures. Napoleon III commissioned some models as present for French Army officers.

British Prime Minister William Ewart Gladstone showed his Blanchet timepiece to Camillo Benso, count of Cavour, the leading figure in the movement toward Italian unification.

References

- Watchmakers & Clockmakers of the World, G.H. Baillie, Nag Press, Vol. 1 (1951).

External links

- Official website [1]

Juvenia

Juvenia

Type	Owned by Asia Commercial Holdings Ltd.
Founded	Saint-Imier, Switzerland (1860)
Founder(s)	Jacques Didisheim-Goldschmidt
Headquarters	La Chaux-de-Fonds, Switzerland
Products	Watches
Website	http://www.juvenia.com/

Juvenia is a luxury Swiss watch manufacturer located in La Chaux-de-Fonds, Switzerland. It is one of the few Swiss watch companies to have manufactured watches without interruption since its creation. The brand is currently owned by Hong Kong group Asia Commercial Holdings Ltd.

History

Juvenia was founded in 1860 by Jacques Didisheim-Goldschmidt in Saint-Imier, Switzerland. Shortly after he relocated to La Chaux-de-Fonds, expecting better opportunities. Jacques' son, Bernard, later succeeded his father.

In the 1880's, Juvenia produced one of the first ladies wristwatches. In 1914, Juvenia manufactured, at the time, the smallest movement constructed on a single level.

Juvenia is known for its extraordinary, avant-garde, case designs, unusual time indications and architectural inspiration.

In 1988, Juvenia was acquired by Asia Commercial Holdings Ltd.

Watch models

A selection:

- Mystère - 1940
- Excentrique - Curved case equipped with a quartz movement
- Retro Automatic
- Arithmo - wristwatch, pocket- watch or desk clock (1945)
- Trigone - large triangular hands (1950's)
- Slimatic

External links

- Official site [1]

Christian Jacques

Christian Jacques

Type	Subsidiary of Jean-Paul Luttenauer AG
Industry	Watch manufacturing
Founded	1988 by Christian Bach & Jacques Geeraerts
Headquarters	Basel, Switzerland
Key people	Jean-Paul Luttenauer, CEO
Products	Wrist watches
Parent	J.-P. Luttenauer AG
Website	www.christian-jacques.com [1]

Christian Jacques is a Swiss brand of watches based in Basel (Switzerland), home to the world's largest watch fair: BaselWorld. Christian Jacques is also one of the last independent brands in the Swiss watch industry.

History

Founded in 1988 by two friends sharing a passion for the art of watch-making, Christian Bach and Jacques Geeraerts, the brand Christian Jacques has expanded significantly since 1995, the year Jean-Paul Luttenauer (current CEO) bought it.

Christian Jacques produces its timepieces in Bulle, Switzerland, with the highest level of traditional Swiss craftsmanship and under the very strict Swiss Made label. Their watches are available on many markets such as Switzerland, European Union, Russia, Ukraine, Azerbaijan, the United Arab Emirates, Qatar, the Gulf States. Hong Kong, People's Republic of China, Macao and Singapore have been added more recently.

Watch Models

Offering the very best Switzerland has to offer but at sensible prices, Christian Jacques turns dreams into reality by offering elegant Swiss Made timepieces for men and women with a sharp sense of esthetic into designs, and a commitment for extreme reliability.

Their range goes from stainless steel quartz model to exclusive limited editions in solid rose gold (18k) with automatic Valjoux movement, and other refined timepieces with set diamonds, High-Tech ceramics, carbon fibers and other noble materials.

Christian Jacques releases one or two new models per year, on top of its already short series, limited editions and various models and versions with own original designs.

Men collection:

- Aviator
- Cubus
- Explorator
- Magister
- Magnus
- Oceanus
- Virtus

Ladies collection:

- Ceramica
- Ignis
- Stella

Limited Edition:

- Eos / 100 pcs
- Ceramagna / 500 pcs

Corporate identity

Christian Jacques has greatly modernized its corporate identity in 2009 with new display materials, new refined packagings and catalogs.

End of 2009, after over 20 years of success and fast growth without any other advertisement that satisfied customers, the brand has armed itself with an impressive advertising material, to support its new operations across Asia-Pacific.

References

- http://www.swisstime.ch/pgs/rwi-pgs-entr-lgs-en-ide-841-zp-zone_info_en.html
- http://www.watch-wow.com/christian-jacques-turning-dreams-into-reality/
- http://www.sunnywatches.com/watches/christian-jacques.html
- http://www.geekwatches.com/category/christian-jacques
- http://watches.infoniac.com/eos-christian-jacques-watch-best.html
- http://www.swwatch.com/index.php?ukey=news&blog_id=560
- http://www.toffsworld.com/fashion/watch-makers/baselworld-luxury-watchmakers-latest-designs/
- http://www.whitelinehotels.com/blog/basel-watch-fair/
- http://watch-happening.blogspot.com/2009/03/baselworld-2009-christian-jacques.html
- http://www.hour-hand.com/index.php/Christian-Jacques/
- http://www.luhho.com/index.php?format=html&Itemid=85&option=com_content&view=article&catid=22:luhho&id=817:baselworld-2010-christian-
- http://www.adensya.ru/guide/pj-watches
- http://www.hk-pub.com/forum/thread-2821900-1-1.html
- http://theescapement.blogspot.com/2010/02/baselworld-2010-preview-pt-iv.html
- http://baselcatalog.messe.ch/mch/zoomdetails_search.asp?exhibitor=113884
- http://www.linternaute.com/homme/mode-accessoires/montres-baselworld-2010/christian-jacques.shtml
- http://www.wristwatchhaven.com/christian-jacques/christian-jacques-eos-chronograph-wristwatch/
- http://watch-wiki.de/index.php?title=Jean-Paul_Luttenauer_AG

External links

- Official website [1]

Article Sources and Contributors

The Swatch Group *Source*: http://en.wikipedia.org/?oldid=390029596 *Contributors*: 1 anonymous edits

Rolex *Source*: http://en.wikipedia.org/?oldid=387896851 *Contributors*:

International Watch Company *Source*: http://en.wikipedia.org/?oldid=386052120 *Contributors*:

Tissot *Source*: http://en.wikipedia.org/?oldid=388858733 *Contributors*: Sprinter77

Waltham Watch Company *Source*: http://en.wikipedia.org/?oldid=381829557 *Contributors*:

Waltham International *Source*: http://en.wikipedia.org/?oldid=379559202 *Contributors*: Auntof6

Breitling *Source*: http://en.wikipedia.org/?oldid=388198961 *Contributors*: Kgasso

Omega SA *Source*: http://en.wikipedia.org/?oldid=389436938 *Contributors*: TheObsidianFriar

TAG Heuer *Source*: http://en.wikipedia.org/?oldid=388487510 *Contributors*: 1 anonymous edits

Patek Philippe & Co. *Source*: http://en.wikipedia.org/?oldid=390058568 *Contributors*: 1 anonymous edits

Vacheron Constantin *Source*: http://en.wikipedia.org/?oldid=385438457 *Contributors*: 1 anonymous edits

Piaget SA *Source*: http://en.wikipedia.org/?oldid=390124936 *Contributors*: Δ

Valjoux *Source*: http://en.wikipedia.org/?oldid=384194566 *Contributors*: 1 anonymous edits

Zeno-Watch Basel *Source*: http://en.wikipedia.org/?oldid=385990802 *Contributors*: Racklever

Zenith (watchmaker) *Source*: http://en.wikipedia.org/?oldid=390439582 *Contributors*:

Baume et Mercier *Source*: http://en.wikipedia.org/?oldid=378893487 *Contributors*:

Movado *Source*: http://en.wikipedia.org/?oldid=387992672 *Contributors*:

Ulysse Nardin *Source*: http://en.wikipedia.org/?oldid=390499822 *Contributors*: Lamro

Chopard *Source*: http://en.wikipedia.org/?oldid=384811238 *Contributors*: 1 anonymous edits

Audemars Piguet *Source*: http://en.wikipedia.org/?oldid=388455801 *Contributors*:

Titoni *Source*: http://en.wikipedia.org/?oldid=336775656 *Contributors*:

Franck Muller *Source*: http://en.wikipedia.org/?oldid=389696999 *Contributors*: Robomod

Rotary Watches *Source*: http://en.wikipedia.org/?oldid=382511835 *Contributors*: 1 anonymous edits

Rado (watch) *Source*: http://en.wikipedia.org/?oldid=381594078 *Contributors*: Qsecofr

Invicta Watch Group *Source*: http://en.wikipedia.org/?oldid=389386310 *Contributors*: 1 anonymous edits

Alpina Watches *Source*: http://en.wikipedia.org/?oldid=335120861 *Contributors*: Rich Farmbrough

Jaeger-LeCoultre *Source*: http://en.wikipedia.org/?oldid=379520601 *Contributors*: 1 anonymous edits

Ollech & Wajs *Source*: http://en.wikipedia.org/?oldid=367464619 *Contributors*: Davidbspalding

Hublot *Source*: http://en.wikipedia.org/?oldid=388434743 *Contributors*: 1 anonymous edits

Eterna *Source*: http://en.wikipedia.org/?oldid=388540310 *Contributors*: 1 anonymous edits

Jovial (watch) *Source*: http://en.wikipedia.org/?oldid=335002561 *Contributors*: 1 anonymous edits

Greubel Forsey *Source*: http://en.wikipedia.org/?oldid=386372551 *Contributors*: Ukexpat

Gallet & Co. *Source*: http://en.wikipedia.org/?oldid=386678653 *Contributors*: Rich Farmbrough

Wyler (company) *Source*: http://en.wikipedia.org/?oldid=385033906 *Contributors*: 1 anonymous edits

Armand Nicolet *Source*: http://en.wikipedia.org/?oldid=380009646 *Contributors*: 1 anonymous edits

Sandoz watches *Source*: http://en.wikipedia.org/?oldid=348315447 *Contributors*: Moonraker2

Mido (watch) *Source*: http://en.wikipedia.org/?oldid=366573817 *Contributors*:

mb-microtec *Source*: http://en.wikipedia.org/?oldid=367844984 *Contributors*: A930913

Roamer (watchmaker) *Source*: http://en.wikipedia.org/?oldid=348984222 *Contributors*: Andy Dingley

Société Suisse pour l'Industrie Horlogère *Source*: http://en.wikipedia.org/?oldid=376427750 *Contributors*: Rjwilmsi

Allgemeine Gesellschaft der schweizerischen Uhrenindustrie AG *Source*: http://en.wikipedia.org/?oldid=381580215 *Contributors*: Pointillist

General Watch Co *Source*: http://en.wikipedia.org/?oldid=370624684 *Contributors*: Claude girardin

Société de Microélectronique et d'Horlogerie *Source*: http://en.wikipedia.org/?oldid=311996280 *Contributors*: Oddharmonic

Endura Watch Factory *Source*: http://en.wikipedia.org/?oldid=320526150 *Contributors*:

TechnoMarine *Source*: http://en.wikipedia.org/?oldid=385800146 *Contributors*: Racklever

West End Watch Co *Source*: http://en.wikipedia.org/?oldid=385800319 *Contributors*: Racklever

Romain Gauthier *Source*: http://en.wikipedia.org/?oldid=349482005 *Contributors*: Katharineamy

Zodiac Watches *Source*: http://en.wikipedia.org/?oldid=355170267 *Contributors*: Colonies Chris

Mathey-Tissot *Source*: http://en.wikipedia.org/?oldid=366592457 *Contributors*:

Blanchet (watch) *Source*: http://en.wikipedia.org/?oldid=387203714 *Contributors*:

Juvenia *Source*: http://en.wikipedia.org/?oldid=382890915 *Contributors*: Akerans

Christian Jacques *Source*: http://en.wikipedia.org/?oldid=387753385 *Contributors*: Funandtrvl

Image Sources, Licenses and Contributors

File:Flik Flak.jpg *Source*: http://en.wikipedia.org/w/index.php?title=File:Flik_Flak.jpg *License*: Creative Commons Attribution-Sharealike 3.0 *Contributors*: User:Khalid Mahmood

File:Swatch Once Again.jpg *Source*: http://en.wikipedia.org/w/index.php?title=File:Swatch_Once_Again.jpg *License*: Creative Commons Attribution-Sharealike 3.0 *Contributors*: User:Khalid Mahmood

File:The Rolex Submariner Professional.JPG *Source*: http://en.wikipedia.org/w/index.php?title=File:The_Rolex_Submariner_Professional.JPG *License*: Creative Commons Attribution-Sharealike 2.5 *Contributors*: User:Tasoskessaris

File:RolexDaytona.jpg *Source*: http://en.wikipedia.org/w/index.php?title=File:RolexDaytona.jpg *License*: GNU Free Documentation License *Contributors*: Jalo, Ptraister

File:Rolex deepsea.jpg *Source*: http://en.wikipedia.org/w/index.php?title=File:Rolex_deepsea.jpg *License*: GNU Free Documentation License *Contributors*: Original uploader was Ruegger at en.wikipedia

File:P1010380.JPG *Source*: http://en.wikipedia.org/w/index.php?title=File:P1010380.JPG *License*: Creative Commons Attribution-Sharealike 2.5 *Contributors*: en:user:Suhailb

File:Cosmo.jpg *Source*: http://en.wikipedia.org/w/index.php?title=File:Cosmo.jpg *License*: Public Domain *Contributors*: Original uploader was Rastapopoulos at en.wikipedia

Image:Rolex Geneva 2.jpg *Source*: http://en.wikipedia.org/w/index.php?title=File:Rolex_Geneva_2.jpg *License*: Creative Commons Attribution-Sharealike 2.5 *Contributors*: user:Nicolas Ray

Image:Rolex Bienne 03.jpg *Source*: http://en.wikipedia.org/w/index.php?title=File:Rolex_Bienne_03.jpg *License*: Creative Commons Attribution-Sharealike 2.5 *Contributors*: User:Oblic

Image:MIH-film116jpg.jpg *Source*: http://en.wikipedia.org/w/index.php?title=File:MIH-film116jpg.jpg *License*: Creative Commons Attribution-Sharealike 2.0 *Contributors*: User:Rama

Image:International Watch Company Manufacture.jpg *Source*: http://en.wikipedia.org/w/index.php?title=File:International_Watch_Company_Manufacture.jpg *License*: Public Domain *Contributors*: User:Prunk

Image:Portugaise IWC.jpg *Source*: http://en.wikipedia.org/w/index.php?title=File:Portugaise_IWC.jpg *License*: Creative Commons Attribution-Sharealike 2.0 *Contributors*: User:Rama

Image:MIH-film121jpg.jpg *Source*: http://en.wikipedia.org/w/index.php?title=File:MIH-film121jpg.jpg *License*: Creative Commons Attribution-Sharealike 2.0 *Contributors*: User:Rama

Image:IWC GST ref. 3707 - dial.jpg *Source*: http://en.wikipedia.org/w/index.php?title=File:IWC_GST_ref._3707_-_dial.jpg *License*: Public Domain *Contributors*: User:Jacob Seligmann

File:IWC Big Pilot St Exupery edition.JPG *Source*: http://en.wikipedia.org/w/index.php?title=File:IWC_Big_Pilot_St_Exupery_edition.JPG *License*: Creative Commons Attribution-Sharealike 3.0 *Contributors*: User:Ferengi

File:HK TST Night 1881 Heritage Shop IWC Schaffhausen 2.JPG *Source*: http://en.wikipedia.org/w/index.php?title=File:HK_TST_Night_1881_Heritage_Shop_IWC_Schaffhausen_2.JPG *License*: Creative Commons Attribution-Sharealike 3.0 *Contributors*: User:A22Empa

File:TissotLeLocle.jpg *Source*: http://en.wikipedia.org/w/index.php?title=File:TissotLeLocle.jpg *License*: Public Domain *Contributors*: TheUrsus

File:Tissotwatchtouch.jpg *Source*: http://en.wikipedia.org/w/index.php?title=File:Tissotwatchtouch.jpg *License*: unknown *Contributors*: FDV

Image:WalthamWatchCompany.jpg *Source*: http://en.wikipedia.org/w/index.php?title=File:WalthamWatchCompany.jpg *License*: Public Domain *Contributors*: Karel K., Midnightdreary, Struthious Bandersnatch

Image:Waltham Watch Company advertisement, 1913.png *Source*: http://en.wikipedia.org/w/index.php?title=File:Waltham_Watch_Company_advertisement,_1913.png *License*: Public Domain *Contributors*: Karel K., Struthious Bandersnatch

Image:Breitling-Navitimer.jpg *Source*: http://en.wikipedia.org/w/index.php?title=File:Breitling-Navitimer.jpg *License*: unknown *Contributors*: Torsten Bolten

Image:Breitling MG 2705.jpg *Source*: http://en.wikipedia.org/w/index.php?title=File:Breitling_MG_2705.jpg *License*: Creative Commons Attribution-Sharealike 2.0 *Contributors*: User:Rama

Image:Breitling_for_Bentley_Motors.jpg *Source*: http://en.wikipedia.org/w/index.php?title=File:Breitling_for_Bentley_Motors.jpg *License*: unknown *Contributors*: AldoOriginal uploader was Totalaldo at en.wikipedia

Image:Super_Avenger_1.jpg *Source*: http://en.wikipedia.org/w/index.php?title=File:Super_Avenger_1.jpg *License*: Creative Commons Attribution-Sharealike 2.5 *Contributors*: Original uploader was Hardee17 at en.wikipedia

Image:Super_Avenger_2.jpg *Source*: http://en.wikipedia.org/w/index.php?title=File:Super_Avenger_2.jpg *License*: Creative Commons Attribution-Sharealike 2.5 *Contributors*: Original uploader was Hardee17 at en.wikipedia

Image:Omega Logo.svg *Source*: http://en.wikipedia.org/w/index.php?title=File:Omega_Logo.svg *License*: Trademarked *Contributors*: Omega

File:Workspace of Louis Brandt.jpg *Source*: http://en.wikipedia.org/w/index.php?title=File:Workspace_of_Louis_Brandt.jpg *License*: Creative Commons Attribution 3.0 *Contributors*: User:Sandstein

Image:Omega medical 2.jpg *Source*: http://en.wikipedia.org/w/index.php?title=File:Omega_medical_2.jpg *License*: Public Domain *Contributors*: Time Maven

Image:Omega Seamaster De Ville 1970.jpg *Source*: http://en.wikipedia.org/w/index.php?title=File:Omega_Seamaster_De_Ville_1970.jpg *License*: Public Domain *Contributors*: Fourdee

Image:OMEGA-Speedmaster-Professional-Front.jpg *Source*: http://en.wikipedia.org/w/index.php?title=File:OMEGA-Speedmaster-Professional-Front.jpg *License*: Public Domain *Contributors*: Torsten Bolten

Image:Bond-Omega.JPG *Source*: http://en.wikipedia.org/w/index.php?title=File:Bond-Omega.JPG *License*: Public Domain *Contributors*: Original uploader was FrankWilliams at en.wikipedia

Image:Planetocean.jpg *Source*: http://en.wikipedia.org/w/index.php?title=File:Planetocean.jpg *License*: Public Domain *Contributors*: Original uploader was Redboard99 at en.wikipedia

File:Loudspeaker.svg *Source*: http://en.wikipedia.org/w/index.php?title=File:Loudspeaker.svg *License*: Public Domain *Contributors*: Bayo, Gmaxwell, Husky, Iamunknown, Myself488, Nethac DIU, Omegatron, Rocket000, The Evil IP address, Wouterhagens, 10 anonymous edits

Image:Heuer Autavia 1962.jpg *Source*: http://en.wikipedia.org/w/index.php?title=File:Heuer_Autavia_1962.jpg *License*: Public Domain *Contributors*: User:Jeff stein

Image:Heuer Carrera 1964.jpg *Source*: http://en.wikipedia.org/w/index.php?title=File:Heuer_Carrera_1964.jpg *License*: Public Domain *Contributors*: User:Jeff stein

File:TAG Heuer Monaco 40th Anniversary re-edition.JPG *Source*: http://en.wikipedia.org/w/index.php?title=File:TAG_Heuer_Monaco_40th_Anniversary_re-edition.JPG *License*: Creative Commons Attribution-Sharealike 3.0 *Contributors*: User:Ferengi

Image:6 grand fo this beotch.jpg *Source*: http://en.wikipedia.org/w/index.php?title=File:6_grand_fo_this_beotch.jpg *License*: Public Domain *Contributors*: User:Malken00

Image:Patek-Philippe MG 2584.jpg *Source*: http://en.wikipedia.org/w/index.php?title=File:Patek-Philippe_MG_2584.jpg *License*: Creative Commons Attribution-Sharealike 2.0 *Contributors*: User:Rama

Image:Patek-Philippe MG 2596.jpg *Source*: http://en.wikipedia.org/w/index.php?title=File:Patek-Philippe_MG_2596.jpg *License*: Creative Commons Attribution-Sharealike 2.0 *Contributors*: User:Rama

Image:Patek-Philippe MG 2586.jpg *Source*: http://en.wikipedia.org/w/index.php?title=File:Patek-Philippe_MG_2586.jpg *License*: Creative Commons Attribution-Sharealike 2.0 *Contributors*: User:Rama

Image:Patek-Philippe MG 2583.jpg *Source*: http://en.wikipedia.org/w/index.php?title=File:Patek-Philippe_MG_2583.jpg *License*: Creative Commons Attribution-Sharealike 2.0 *Contributors*: User:Rama

Image:patekphillipe2-wiki-g.png *Source*: http://en.wikipedia.org/w/index.php?title=File:Patekphillipe2-wiki-g.png *License*: Creative Commons Attribution-Sharealike 2.5 *Contributors*: Jamin, ZyMOS, 2 anonymous edits

Image:Patekphillipe-inside-wiki2-g.png *Source*: http://en.wikipedia.org/w/index.php?title=File:Patekphillipe-inside-wiki2-g.png *License*: Creative Commons Attribution-Sharealike 2.5 *Contributors*: Jamin, ZyMOS

Image:Calatrava1.jpg *Source*: http://en.wikipedia.org/w/index.php?title=File:Calatrava1.jpg *License*: Public Domain *Contributors*: User:Jeff Muscato. Original uploader was Jeff Muscato at en.wikipedia

Image:Valjoux7750.JPG *Source*: http://en.wikipedia.org/w/index.php?title=File:Valjoux7750.JPG *License*: Creative Commons Zero *Contributors*: User:Ofbarea

Image:Montre-Zeno-p1020456.jpg *Source*: http://en.wikipedia.org/w/index.php?title=File:Montre-Zeno-p1020456.jpg *License*: Creative Commons Attribution-Sharealike 2.0 *Contributors*: User:Rama

Image:MIH-film126jpg.jpg *Source*: http://en.wikipedia.org/w/index.php?title=File:MIH-film126jpg.jpg *License*: Creative Commons Attribution-Sharealike 2.0 *Contributors*: User:Rama

File:Zenith img 0988.jpg *Source*: http://en.wikipedia.org/w/index.php?title=File:Zenith_img_0988.jpg *License*: Creative Commons Attribution-Sharealike 2.0 *Contributors*: User:Rama

File:Zenit img 0985.jpg *Source*: http://en.wikipedia.org/w/index.php?title=File:Zenit_img_0985.jpg *License*: Creative Commons Attribution-Sharealike 2.0 *Contributors*: User:Rama

File:Zenith img 0987.jpg *Source*: http://en.wikipedia.org/w/index.php?title=File:Zenith_img_0987.jpg *License*: Creative Commons Attribution-Sharealike 2.0 *Contributors*: User:Rama

Image:Beaume and Mercier watch.jpg *Source*: http://en.wikipedia.org/w/index.php?title=File:Beaume_and_Mercier_watch.jpg *License*: unknown *Contributors*: User:Rama

Image:malibuwatch.jpg *Source*: http://en.wikipedia.org/w/index.php?title=File:Malibuwatch.jpg *License*: Creative Commons Attribution-Sharealike 3.0 *Contributors*: User:Zero1975

Image:LeRoy01.jpg *Source*: http://en.wikipedia.org/w/index.php?title=File:LeRoy01.jpg *License*: Creative Commons Attribution-Sharealike 3.0 *Contributors*: User:Zero1975

Image:Ulysse-Nardin MG 2569.jpg *Source*: http://en.wikipedia.org/w/index.php?title=File:Ulysse-Nardin_MG_2569.jpg *License*: Creative Commons Attribution-Sharealike 2.0 *Contributors*: User:Rama

Image:Ulysse-Nardin MG 2565.jpg *Source*: http://en.wikipedia.org/w/index.php?title=File:Ulysse-Nardin_MG_2565.jpg *License*: Creative Commons Attribution-Sharealike 2.0 *Contributors*: User:Rama

Image:Ulysse-Nardin MG 2566.jpg *Source*: http://en.wikipedia.org/w/index.php?title=File:Ulysse-Nardin_MG_2566.jpg *License*: Creative Commons Attribution-Sharealike 2.0 *Contributors*: User:Rama

Image:UlysseNardin.jpg *Source*: http://en.wikipedia.org/w/index.php?title=File:UlysseNardin.jpg *License*: GNU Free Documentation License *Contributors*: Rama, Thebiggestmac

Image:Audemars-Piguet-img 0325.jpg *Source*: http://en.wikipedia.org/w/index.php?title=File:Audemars-Piguet-img_0325.jpg *License*: Creative Commons Attribution-Sharealike 2.0 *Contributors*: User:Rama

Image:Audemars-Piguet-img 0324.jpg *Source*: http://en.wikipedia.org/w/index.php?title=File:Audemars-Piguet-img_0324.jpg *License*: Creative Commons Attribution-Sharealike 2.0 *Contributors*: User:Rama

Image:RadoSilverStar.jpg *Source*: http://en.wikipedia.org/w/index.php?title=File:RadoSilverStar.jpg *License*: Creative Commons Attribution-Sharealike 2.5 *Contributors*: Jamin, Zckls04

Image:Jaeger Lecoultre img 0992.jpg *Source*: http://en.wikipedia.org/w/index.php?title=File:Jaeger_Lecoultre_img_0992.jpg *License*: Creative Commons Attribution-Sharealike 2.0 *Contributors*: User:Rama

Image:Jaeger-Lecoultre-p1000841.jpg *Source*: http://en.wikipedia.org/w/index.php?title=File:Jaeger-Lecoultre-p1000841.jpg *License*: Creative Commons Attribution-Sharealike 2.0 *Contributors*: User:Rama

File:Atmos img 3422.jpg *Source*: http://en.wikipedia.org/w/index.php?title=File:Atmos_img_3422.jpg *License*: Creative Commons Attribution-Sharealike 2.0 *Contributors*: User:Rama

Image:O_and_w_logo.png *Source*: http://en.wikipedia.org/w/index.php?title=File:O_and_w_logo.png *License*: GNU Free Documentation License *Contributors*: User:LuckyLouie

Image:Ollechandwajsm1.png *Source*: http://en.wikipedia.org/w/index.php?title=File:Ollechandwajsm1.png *License*: Free Art License *Contributors*: User:LuckyLouie

Image:Greubel Forsey Logo 08.jpg *Source*: http://en.wikipedia.org/w/index.php?title=File:Greubel_Forsey_Logo_08.jpg *License*: Creative Commons Attribution 3.0 *Contributors*: Greubel Forsey. Original uploader was Underthedial at en.wikipedia

Image:Greubel Forsey DT20 Vision.jpg *Source*: http://en.wikipedia.org/w/index.php?title=File:Greubel_Forsey_DT20_Vision.jpg *License*: Creative Commons Attribution 3.0 *Contributors*: greubel Forsey

File:Flag of Switzerland.svg *Source*: http://en.wikipedia.org/w/index.php?title=File:Flag_of_Switzerland.svg *License*: Public Domain *Contributors*: User:-xfi-, User:Marc Mongenet, User:Zscout370

File:WE-Building.jpg *Source*: http://en.wikipedia.org/w/index.php?title=File:WE-Building.jpg *License*: GNU Free Documentation License *Contributors*: CINDY1983

Image:Zodiac-logo.png *Source*: http://en.wikipedia.org/w/index.php?title=File:Zodiac-logo.png *License*: Public Domain *Contributors*: Albedo-ukr, Cwbm (commons), Gridge, Latics, Perhelion, 1 anonymous edits

File:E. Mathey-Tissot minute-repeater, c. 1909.jpg *Source*: http://en.wikipedia.org/w/index.php?title=File:E._Mathey-Tissot_minute-repeater,_c._1909.jpg *License*: Creative Commons Attribution-Sharealike 2.5 *Contributors*: Mathey-Tissot

File:Mathey-tissot calamatic 1947.jpg *Source*: http://en.wikipedia.org/w/index.php?title=File:Mathey-tissot_calamatic_1947.jpg *License*: Creative Commons Attribution-Sharealike 2.5 *Contributors*: Mathey-Tissot

Image:Blanchet logo.jpg *Source*: http://en.wikipedia.org/w/index.php?title=File:Blanchet_logo.jpg *License*: unknown *Contributors*: blanchetwatches.com

CPSIA information can be obtained at www.ICGtesting.com
Printed in the USA
LVOW111549290113

317738LV00009B/544/P

9 781242 788215